PREVENTING SUICIDE: CLOSING THE EXITS REVISITED

PREVENTING SUICIDE: CLOSING THE EXITS REVISITED

DAVID LESTER

Nova Science Publishers, Inc.
New York

LIBRARY OF CONGRESS CATALOGING-IN-PUBLICATION DATA
Lester, David, 1942-
  Preventing suicide : closing the exits revisited / David Lester.
    p. cm.
  Includes bibliographical references and index.
  ISBN 978-1-60741-360-8 (hardcover : alk. paper)
  1. Suicide--Prevention. 2. Suicide. 3. Suicidal behavior. I. Title.
  HV6545.L4197   2009
  362.28'7--dc22
                                                                          2009014717

Published by Nova Science Publishers, Inc. ✦ New York

CONTENTS

PREFACE

In 1989, Ronald Clarke and I published a book entitled *Suicide: Closing the Exits* in which we reported research that we had conducted, individually and together, on the impact of restricting access to lethal methods of suicide on the suicide rate. Ronald Clarke had a background in criminology and crime prevention, while I had a background in suicidology and suicide prevention. We reported the results of our own research on the impact of the detoxification of domestic gas, the toxicity of car exhaust, and firearm availability on suicide. Did restricting access to lethal methods of suicide prevent suicide? We concluded that in many, but not all, cases it did.

In the twenty years since then, a great deal of research has appeared on this issue, and the present book reviews this research. My goal is to survey what we have learned about six specific ways of restricting access to methods for suicide: domestic gas, car exhaust, jumping from bridges and high buildings, jumping in front of trains and subway cars, medication and poisons (including pesticides), and (for some countries) firearms. This book does not review the research on controlling access to firearms in the United States. This topic has not only generated the most research, but the research has been contentious since it has social and political implications. As a result, this important topic will be covered in a separate book which is presently in progress.

The idea for this book came from Professors Graeme Newman and Ronald Clarke who encouraged me to write it. Unfortunately, it was not possible to fit the book into the series of texts that they were preparing. Preliminary versions of some of these chapters have appeared in the *Journal of Islamic Countries Organization of Forensic Medicine*, and I would like to thank the Islamic Organization of Forensic Medicine for their support in publishing my essays.

Chapter 1

INTRODUCTION

There have been many approaches proposed and implemented for preventing suicide. Restricting access to lethal methods is only one. In this introductory chapter, I will briefly review these approaches.

THE ROLE OF THE GOVERNMENT

Some of the goals of a public health approach to suicide prevention involve the government. With regard to suicide prevention, the United States government has played a small role. Funding for research into suicide has come from the National Institute for Mental Health (and other institutes) and from the National Science Foundation. For a few years, NIMH had a special section for suicidology (Shneidman, 1967), which produced a journal called the *Bulletin of Suicidology*, beginning in 1967, with eight issues (and a supplement on youth suicide) until it ceased publication in 1971. A government task force on youth suicide was established with a report published in 1989, and since then there has been a report from the Surgeon General in 1999, a report from the Institute of Medicine in 2002, and some increase in funding. The United Nations and the World Health Organization have also focused on suicide prevention in recent years.

The United States federal government collects mortality statistics and makes them available in printed summaries and, now, on data tapes. Since 1933, data have been provided for the whole nation, and this permits studies of the epidemiology of suicide. More recently, the Centers for Disease Control has published the *Morbidity and Mortality Weekly Report* which contains articles on current trends in mortality and in physical and psychiatric illnesses, including suicide, and occasional articles on guidelines for handling suicidal situations, such as the aftermath of suicides which occur in schools and the reporting of suicides by the media. The Centers for Disease Control is presently focusing on injury prevention and sponsoring conferences, publications (such as *Injury Control Update*) and research in order to catch the attention of both professionals and the general public.

This information-dissemination approach can galvanize public and political support for preventive efforts, but these efforts are sometimes opposed by other groups in the society. For example, although strict gun control might well reduce the use of firearms for suicide, organizations such as the National Rifle Association oppose laws which strengthen gun control laws or which ban guns. Scholarly research is not, therefore, sufficient to produce changes at the government level. Public opinion must be marshalled in order to overcome the pressures exerted by those opposed to the necessary changes.

The major professional association concerned with suicide prevention in the United States is the American Association of Suicidology, founded in 1968 (Swenson, 1968), which holds annual meetings, publishes a scholarly journal and newsletters, and brings together scholars, crisis intervention workers and survivors (those who have lost a loved one to suicide). The association also accredits suicide prevention and crisis intervention services and offers a national examination for crisis counselors.

These kinds of government and professional activities are relevant to a public health approach. Interestingly, Lester (1992) found that the states in America which had developed programs to combat youth suicide had improved their youth suicide rates relative to states which had taken little or no action. Thus, concern about suicide at the government level may have a beneficial impact on the communities they serve.

EDUCATION PROGRAMS

Education programs have focused on two groups: school children and physicians.

School Programs

School suicide prevention programs have focused primarily on educating students about the risk factors for identifying suicidal students, changing attitudes toward suicide so that the topic can be discussed in a more supportive manner, and encouraging appropriate responses to suicidal peers. Many of the programs, therefore, seem oriented toward turning all students into potential crisis counselors.

Ryerson (1990) has developed a more comprehensive program in which the goal is to raise the level of awareness and knowledge in all members of the school community -- students, staff and parents. Her program covers such issues as the warning signs for suicidal adolescents, the epidemiology of adolescent suicide, the different face of depression in adolescents, the causes of adolescent suicide, what educators, parents and peers can do to help those in suicidal crises, and what community resources exist.

Ryerson's program involves (1) a three-hour intensive seminar for school staff (including teachers, administrators and all support staff including the cafeteria and maintenance workers, coaches and secretaries), (2) a variety of parent programs, ranging from thirty minutes to two hours, and (3) four to six hour student workshops which can be incorporated into the teaching curriculum. It is important to provide adequate mental health care in the community to handle students who are identified as suicidal and who are referred for more sustained treatment. Ryerson's goal is to make the program an on-going one in which the school staff take over running the workshops after a couple of years.

Not all commentators in this field agree that such programs are beneficial. There has been doubts raised about whether the programs reduce the incidence of suicidal behaviors and whether the programs for students might distress and increase the risk of suicide for some students (Shaffer et al., 1988). Ryerson stresses the importance of evaluating these programs, and several evaluation studies have appeared in recent years. For example, Kalafat and Elias (1994) found positive impacts from a general suicide awareness program for adolescents, Eggert et al. (1995) found that a treatment program for school children identified as at risk for suicide was beneficial for the children, and Mackesy-Amiti et al. (1996) found that a program for educators increased their knowledge about suicide in adolescents. Ciffone (2007) has replicated these successes in recently, but the impact of these remains on suicidal behavior *per se* remains undocumented. [1]

Educating Physicians

Rutz et al. (1989) have shown that a program to educate physicians in the detection, evaluation and appropriate treatment of depression and suicide led to a reduction in the suicide rate on the island of Gotland (Sweden) as compared to the rest of Sweden. Eventually, without continued training, especially for physicians new to the island, the suicide rate rose again.[2] Marshall (1971) trained community nurses in a rural area to recognize suicidal risk in their clients, but he did not evaluate the effectiveness of the program.

Whereas this intensive post-graduate education had a beneficial impact on suicidal behavior, simple warnings probably do not work. For example, Soumerai et al. (1987) found that warning physicians about the misuse of Darvon had no impact on the death rate from Darvon. On the other hand, "black box" warnings on medications may have an impact on prescribing practices by psychiatrists and other physicians. Warnings about the risk of suicide in adolescents for whom the SSRI anti-depressants were prescribed had a significant impact of prescribing practices in Great Britain and the United States, but not in Canada (Kurdyak et al., 2007; Lineberry et al, 2007)

Educating the Media

It has been clearly demonstrated that media publicity about the suicides of celebrities results in an increase in the suicide rate for the next week at least (Stack, 1990). Thus, care should be taken by the media in how they present news about suicides so that imitation is minimized. For example, publishing details of the method used and how it was obtained is dangerous. Glamorizing the suicide is likely to increase the suggestive impact of the suicide on others. Furthermore, researchers in the field have suggested that the media should always accompany suicide stories with information about suicide prevention resources in the community (Centers for Disease Control, 1988).

---

[1] Programs have also been developed to provide crisis intervention to schools after a student has committed suicide (Wenckstern & Leenaars, 1991).

[2] Recently, Zonda et al. (2006-2007) failed to replicate this result in Budapest, Hungary.

IMPROVING MENTAL HEALTH SERVICE DELIVERY

There are several tactics which appear to have potential for preventing suicide, whose effectiveness depends in part on improving the delivery of particular services to the general public, a public health concern.

Medical Emergency Services

Diggory (undated) argued that we are preventing suicide with our emergency medical procedures. He estimated that in 1971, for example, the suicide rate in Pittsburgh was reduced from 15.2 to 12.5 (a reduction of 18 percent) simply by saving the lives of those who had attempted suicide. Thus, an improvement in emergency medical care would probably increase the extent to which those who might have died from their suicidal actions would survive. However, in the United States at the present time, while the medical treatment of seriously-injured people has improved, emergency room services are closing down in some rural areas as hospitals attempt to increase profits (or minimize losses), a policy which limits the ability of some communities to save the lives of attempted suicides.

General Mental Health

Prevention of suicide might also focus on providing good general mental health services for communities and for groups with high rates of psychiatric disorder such as aboriginal groups or adolescent runaways. Many years ago Ratcliffe (1962) noted that changing a mental hospital in the United Kingdom from a locked-ward to an open-door system of patient management was accompanied by a drop in the number of suicides in the surrounding community, but a drop in the suicide rate did not always occur when community mental health centers are opened (Walk, 1967). More research is need to identify what factors may affect the success of such programs.

On the other hand, in the United States in recent years, there has been a move to privatize mental health care, to release psychiatric patients from psychiatric institutions, and to reduce the coverage from medical insurance for the treatment of psychiatric disorders. The result is that many former psychiatric patients now live in the community (or on the streets), and those who might benefit from psychiatric treatment and psychotherapy cannot afford it. Thus, increasing access to mental health facilities is not always a realistic goal.

Suicide Prevention Centers

Suicide prevention centers have been set up in many countries in the world, and some have extensive networks of centers so that an individual always has a center near at hand. Suicide prevention centers typically have a 24-hour telephone crisis counseling service staffed by paraprofessional volunteers. Some centers have, in addition, walk-in clinics and emergency out-reach teams which can visit distressed individuals in the community.

This type of suicide prevention has been oriented around a crisis model of the suicidal process. People who are suicidal are conceptualized as being in a time-limited crisis state. Immediate crisis counseling should help the suicidal individual through the suicidal crisis, whereupon a normal life may resume.

Most of these suicide prevention efforts by these centers are essentially passive (Lester, 1989). A suicidal person has to contact the suicide prevention center. Active methods, such as seeking out discharged psychiatric patients, elderly males living alone, and other high risk groups could be undertaken. In addition, physicians as well as community workers such as police officers, clergymen, lawyers, and perhaps groups such as bartenders, prostitutes and hair dressers who also come into contact with the public, could be sensitized to the detection of depressed, disturbed and suicidal people and encouraged to refer them to appropriate resources.

At the present time, three international organizations exist to coordinate suicide prevention centers around the world and to stimulate their development -- Befrienders International, Life Line International and IFOTES (the International Federation of Telephonic Emergency Services). A recent review of the effectiveness of suicide prevention centers in preventing suicide concluded that they do appear to have a small but significant beneficial impact (Lester, 1997).

Treatment for Suicidal Individuals

Treatment for suicidal individuals involves psychotherapy/counseling and medication. The impact of antidepressants on suicide rates was initially controversial, with some commentators arguing that the increased prescribing of antidepressants had not affected societal suicide rates (Van Praag, 2002).

However, recent studies in Finalnd (Korkeila et al., 2007), Sweden (Carlstein et al., 2001) and the United States (Milane et al., 2006) have shown that suicide rates have declined in both countries as the prescription of SSRIs increased. Ludwig and Marcotte (2005), in a study of several nations over time, estimated that an increase of one SSRI pill per capita (a 13% increase over 1999 levels) would reduce the suicide rate by 2.5%.

Although the major systems of psychotherapy have occasionally addressed the issue of counselling suicidal clients (Lester, 1991), their efficacy has not been examined empirically. Cognitive therapy is the major system of psychotherapy recommended widely these days for counselling suicidal clients (e.g., Reinecke & Didie, 2005), and there is some empirical evidence that it helps clients, although its impact on suicidal behavior is less clear. In a review of the clinical management of deliberate self-harm in young people, Burns et al. (2005) found ten studies, one of which provided support for group therapy in reducing the incidence of subsequent self-harm, while another study found success for family therapy in reducing suicidal ideation. Crawford et al. (2007) reviewed 18 studies of psychosocial interventions with clients who had engaged in self-harm behaviors and found no impact on the incidence of subsequent completed suicide. The evidence for the utility of psychotherapy and counselling, therefore, remains unsatisfactory.

SITUATIONAL SUICIDE PREVENTION

Situational suicide prevention has focused on preventing suicide by restricting access to lethal methods for suicide. It involves such tactics as fencing in the places from which people jump to their death (like high buildings and bridges), reducing the toxicity of domestic gas and car exhaust, and restricting the access of people to firearms. The purpose of this book is to review the research on the impact of these restrictions on suicide and to explore whether they reduce the suicide rate or merely force potential suicides to choose alternative methods for suicide. In this introductory chapter, I will review a broader approach to situational suicide prevention, drawing on the work of Wortley (2002), and discuss some preliminary issues.

In explaining human behavior, theorists can take two different approaches: (1) focusing on the personal or intrapsychic variables that cause individuals to behave as they do, or (2) focusing on the environmental stimuli and social forces that elicit behavior from individuals. Of course, the "truth" is that both sets of variables play a role in determining human behavior, but the extreme perspectives lay out the case for each perspective most clearly.

Wortley (2002) explored an environmental point of view, but he construed it broadly, focusing on any aspect of the environment that affects the behavior of individuals. Wortley was interesting in controlling the behavior of prisoners in jails and prisons, and so many of his examples came from that context. If the design of a prison makes it easy for a prisoner to break a glass object (such as a light bulb or a drinking glass) and to produce a glass shard with which to cut himself, then removing access to glass objects is an obvious way of reducing the risk of suicide by this method. But Wortley also considered the possibility that overcrowding in prisons may increase the stress and increase the risk of suicide. Whereas the prisoners and the prison staff are conscious of the role of glass in the prisoners' suicidal behavior, they may not be aware of the role of overcrowding.

Wortley noted that situational tactics are not long-term solutions for suicidal individuals. For example, once the prisoner is released from prison, the situational tactics for preventing suicide in prison are no longer relevant in the outside world. In Wortleys's words, "situational intervention is about creating safe situations rather than creating safe individuals" (p. 4).

There are theories of suicide that are based on an environmental perspective. For example, Lester (1987) proposed a learning theory of suicide in which he examined the roles of such factors as the punishment experiences of childhood, the failure of socialization, the positive and negative reinforcers for suicidal behaviors, contagion, modelling of the suicidal behavior of relatives and significant others, cultural and subcultural factors, societal expectations about when suicide is appropriate, and societal attitudes toward suicide (acceptance versus condemnation). All of these factors would fall into the broad definition of situational factors considered by Wortley in his study of prisoner behavior, but they clearly move far beyond controlling access to lethal methods for suicide. Wortley also considered such situational factors as social influence (including conforming to, obeying and complying with the demands of others), atmospheric conditions, and crowding. For prisons, the focus of his concern, he also included factors such as inmate composition and the turnover of the inmate population.

Wortley made a distinction between situational factors that precipitate or initiate a behavior and those that regulate (that is, inhibit or encourage) the behavior. Situational factors can present stimuli (or cues) that prompt individuals to perform a behavior, exert pressure on individuals to behave in that way, permit individuals to engage in the behavior, and produce emotional arousal that provokes the behavior. Controlling precipitators involves:

- controlling prompts
- controlling pressures
- reducing permissibility
- reducing provocations

Controlling regulators involves:

- increasing the perceived effort
- increasing the perceived risk
- reducing anticipated rewards
- increasing anticipated punishments

Wortley gave examples relevant to controlling violent acts by prisoners. However, examples can be found for suicide prevention. For example, current discussion of suicide bombers focus on how the indoctrination period of training exerts social pressure on the individual to go through with the act, a component of controlling precipitators. The religious prohibitions against suicide and, in the past, laws prohibiting suicide, are examples of ways to increase the anticipated punishment for committing suicide, a component of controlling regulators.

Many scholars in the past have alluded to the role of choice of method in affecting suicide rates, but the notion is usually attributed to Stengel (1964) who discussed the role that the detoxification of domestic gas played in changing national suicide rates. Seiden (1977; Seiden and Spence, 1983-1984) also drew attention to this strategy, noting, for example, that the Golden Gate Bridge in San Francisco was a much more "attractive" suicide locale than the Bay Bridge.

However, the notion that suicide can be prevented by restricting access to lethal methods for suicide is not new. Anderson (1987) documented that, in the 1800s in Victorian England, this tactic was discussed and implemented. In the mid-18th Century, police officers patrolled canals and rivers in which people tried to drown themselves and saved many would-be suicides. Three days after a suicidal jump from the top of the Monument in London in 1842, an iron cage was installed to enclose the viewing gallery. The Highgate Archway was modified similarly in 1897. As early as the 1850s, prisons were being made "safer" by boxing in waterpipes and enclosing galleries with netting to prevent jumping. Anderson also noted that suicides also turned to methods that had become available. Laudanum (a mixture of opiates and alcohol) was a common folk medicine while carbolic acid was used in order to keep houses free from germs. These became common methods for suicide until they were restricted in 1868 (and later in 1908) and 1900, respectively. As photography and home developing became a popular hobby, the use of cyanide for suicide became common and, when penny-slot domestic gas became available in the 1890s, suicide by coal gas became common. A gun control law was introduced in 1893 and passed in 1903, and the percentage of youths using guns for suicide dropped from 20% in 1902 to 15% in 1907.

The first convincing demonstration of the possible effectiveness of this strategy was by Kreitman (1976) who showed that the drop in the English suicide rate was the result of the detoxification of coal gas and the switch to natural gas. The percentage of carbon monoxide in domestic gas declined from 13% in 1955 to 0% in 1975. The suicide rate by carbon monoxide poisoning also declined in all age groups and for both women and men. In contrast, the suicide rate by other methods rose over the same period, but not sufficiently so as to prevent a decline in the overall suicide rate. This early study illustrated the three critical questions involved in good research on the strategy: (1) does the restriction of access to a method for suicide lower the suicide rate by that method, (2) if it does, do people switch to other methods for suicide, and (3) does the overall suicide rate decline?

Clarke and Lester (1989) documented the effectiveness of this approach to suicide prevention. They conducted a number of studies to show that the availability of firearms, toxic car exhaust and toxic domestic gas appears to be strongly related to the use of those methods for suicide, and that reducing the easy availability of these methods for suicide often reduced the overall suicide rate since not everyone switches methods for suicide when their preferred method becomes less easily available. Research relevant to the effectiveness of these tactics for preventing suicide has been reviewed by Lester (1993, 1998), who concluded that the evidence is that they do prevent suicide, although some studies do indicate that switching to alternative methods of suicide does occasionally occur.

Clarke and Lester urged:

> the detoxification of domestic gas,
> limits on the sales and ownership of firearms,
> restricting the size of medication prescriptions,
> placing the pills in plastic blisters which are hard to open,
> adding vomiting-inducing chemicals to medications so that an overdose will
>   result in expulsion of the medication,
> prescription of suppositories rather than orally-taken tablets,
> prescribing the less toxic medications,
> cleaning up car emissions,
> changing the shape of the exhaust pipe to make it difficult to attach tubing,

having an automatic engine turn-off mechanism if the car idles for more than
    a few minutes,
fencing in bridges and high buildings from which people jump, and
restricting the easy availability of herbicides and insecticides in developing
countries.

Related to making the environment safer, another suggestion for suicide prevention is to investigate the environments into which these serious attempters are released. Does their environment contain suicidogenic stresses, hostile significant others who increase the likelihood of self-destructive tendencies, or lethal means for suicide? One suicide prevention center in the United States used to search the homes of attempted suicides, removing all guns, large knives, poisons and lethal drugs. They were able to do this, of course, only for attempted suicides who contacted them, and they did it with the tolerance of the local police force. It is not a technique that is likely to be available to most preventers of suicide, but it does illustrate a technique for "sanitizing the environment."

Applications to Other Social Problems

The notion that restricting access to lethal methods for death might reduce the incidence of the rates of homicide and accidental deaths has also been explored, with results that support the strategy. Lester (1993) reviewed a number of studies on the impact on homicide rates of restricting the availability of firearms and concluded that the evidence for a preventive effect was present but not as strong as that found for suicide. On the other hand, there was less evidence than in the case of suicide for switching to alternative methods for murder when firearms were less available. For accidental deaths, Lester and Abe (1992) found, for example, that the detoxification of domestic gas in both Japan and the United States reduced the accidental death rate from domestic gas.

The strategy has also been extended to other social problems such as the consequences of changing the availability of alcohol on alcohol-related problems (Smith, 1988) and the availability of opportunities for gambling on the incidence of compulsive gambling (Lester, 1994), again with results that support the usefulness of the paradigm.

Many in the field of suicide prevention argue that restricting access to lethal methods for committing suicide is pointless since potential suicides will switch to alternative methods of suicide. I will address this issue by looking at the research data throughout this book to explore the extent to which this switching (often called "displacement") occurs. But it is important to note here that, while there is scepticism about this tactic at the societal, aggregate level, there is widespread acceptance of the tactic at the individual level. For example, if, in a psychiatric hospital, patients are acutely suicidal, placing them in a "suicide proof" environment temporarily, until the suicidal crisis dissipates, is common.

I will, therefore, briefly examine the use of restricting access to lethal methods for committing suicide in prison in the next section.

Suicide Proofing Prison Cells

The tactic of changing the environment so as to reduce the risk of suicide has been employed at the individual level in jails and prisons by redesigning the cells. In this section, I will review some of these proposals.

The vast majority of inmate suicides are the result of hanging. It is not necessary for the victim's feet to be off the ground for death to occur. In fact, only 2 kilograms of pressure is required to obstruct the flow of blood to and from the brain. An adult's head weighs about 3 kilograms, and so a person has only to kneel, stand, sit or even lie down while his neck is in a noose. If the noose is attached to a bar, in order to hang himself, the inmate either quickly spread-eagles, crouches into a prayer-like kneeling position or tucks his legs underneath him in order to add extra weight to the end of the crudely fashioned noose. It takes about 15 minutes to induce total asphyxia, from hooking the noose and cutting off the air supply to cutting off the blood to the head. Brain damage, however, can occur within three minutes. Therefore, jail and prison cells must be examined carefully for possible hooks, from the floor upward.

Stone (1990) examined 107 suicides in Texas jails and found that all but four used hanging. Cloth, shirts, and short strips of material were used in 100 of the 103 hangings. Two others used shoe laces, and one used an extension cord that was in the jail cell in violation of state jail standards.

Stone found that the most common point of attachment was the cell crossbars (35), followed by vent and window grates (21), shower rods (16) and privacy partitions (7). Stone noted that all of these points of attachment can easily be eliminated. Cell bars, grills and grates can be covered with fine mesh metal screens or clear plexiglass sheets. Shower rods and privacy partitions can be removed. Stone also noted that only one of the 16 shower rods used for suicide actually had a shower curtain. Stone recommended that jail administrators should spend an hour in a "suicide-proof" cell and attempt to attach their tie to something 15 or more inches from the floor.

Jordan and co-workers (1987) replaced metal double-bunk beds in the cells in a police station with a single, solid concrete sleeping bench and a flame-retardant mattress. They covered the cell bars with plexiglass which made it impossible to affix strangling materials to the bars. They recessed the ceiling lighting for the same reason. They also installed a sound and video monitoring system to supplement the hourly physical checks by the watch commander.

Atlas (1989) provided a detailed list of suggestions for redesigning cells. For already existing cells, he suggested placing scratch-resistant polycarbonate glazing on the inside of the metal bar doors, modifying the existing light fixtures, putting tamper-proof covers over ventilation openings and all protrusions, removing all electrical outlets and eliminating all exposed pipes, hooks, hinges and catches.

For new cells, Atlas suggested: ceilings 10 feet high; recessed light fixtures and polycarbonate lens coverings; no electrical outlets; fire resistant and nontoxic material for padded walls (if these are permitted by the state); rounded corners for the walls; no exposed pipes, hooks, hinges, door knobs or catches; sealing wall joints with neoprene rubber to prevent gouging through the plaster for the purpose of anchoring a hook; sliding doors to prevent barricading the door or slamming it onto the staff members; solid slab beds; stainless steel toilet sink combinations, concealed piping and outside control over water valves; and fire detectors. To prevent all possibilities of suicide, it is also necessary to have special clothing for inmates that cannot be torn and used for suicide. Paper clothes are one possibility.

Not all inmates commit suicide by hanging. Cutting is sometimes used, and so care must be taken to remove sharp objects with which an inmate could cut or puncture arteries. Potentially dangerous objects, such as pens, are often present in the pockets of correctional staff, and these are often available when an inmate moves about the institution. Thus, they can easily be acquired by inmates if care is not taken. (It is, of course, impossible to prevent regular inmates from having access to such implements.) Porter and Jones (1990) reported the case of an inmate using the lens from his eyeglasses to kill himself.

Other methods used for suicide include fire, jumping and overdosing. Fire can be prevented by removing matches and lighters and using flame-resistant materials in the isolation cells. Jumping can be prevented by fencing in the areas from which inmates might leap or putting netting to catch anyone who jumps. Overdosing on medications can be prevented by using injections, making sure that inmates swallow any pills that they are given, or substituting medications that are less toxic. Henry (1989), for example, calculated the overdose rates per prescription in the general population for major antidepressants, and found that more recently developed antidepressants are less likely to result in suicide.

Some commentators are opposed to "suicide-proofing" cells and to the use of isolation and monitoring. Hayes (1983) has said that these techniques are for the convenience of jail personnel and not for the benefit of the inmate. They increase the chances that the inmate will feel depersonalized. On the other hand, it can be useful (and if often necessary) for an institution to have "suicide-proof" cells available for inmates judged to be high risk. It is, of course, possible to have relatively humanized "suicide-proof" cells. Such cells can be painted warm colors, the bed slab can be colored plastic rather than concrete, there can be music playing, and the inmate can be placed with a cellmate who is a trained suicide prevention worker. It is clear, however, that suicide-proofing cells is a useful component for an effective suicide prevention program in jails and prisons.

CONCLUSION

Suicide-proofing a room can prevent suicidal behavior in incarcerated prisoners and in psychiatric patients. The question addressed in the next seven chapters is whether suicide-proofing the general environment prevents suicide in the general population. The final chapter will sum up the results and discuss the issues stimulated by this body of research.

REFERENCES

Anderson, O. (1987). *Suicide in Victorian and Edwardian England*. Oxford, UK: Clarendon Press.

Atlas, R. (1989). Reducing the opportunities for inmate suicide. *Psychiatric Quarterly*, 60, 161-171.

Burns, J., Dudley, M., Hazell, P., & Patton, G. (2005). Clinical management of deliberate self-harm in young people. *Australian & New Zealand Journal of Psychiatry*, 39, 121-128.

Carlstein, A., Waern, M., Ekedahl, A., & Ranstam, J. (2001). Antidepressant medication and suicide in Sweden. *Pharmacoepidemiology & Drug Safety*, 10, 525-530.

Centers for Disease Control. (1988). CDC recommendations for a community plan for the prevention and containment of suicide clusters. *Morbidity & Mortality Weekly Report*, 37, (supplement # 5-6), 1-12.

Ciffone, J. (2007). Suicide prevention: An analysis and replication of a curriculum-based high school program. *Social Work*, 52, 41-49.

Clarke, R. V., & Lester, D. (1989). *Suicide: Closing the exits*. New York: Springer-Verlag.

Crawford, M. J., Thomas, O., Khan, N., & Kulinskaya, E. (2007). Psychosocial interventions following self-harm. *British Journal of Psychiatry*, 190, 11-17.

Diggory, J. (undated). Empirical evidence for the improved prediction and prevention of suicide. Pittsburgh: Chatham College.

Eggert, L. L., Thompson, E. A., Herting, J. R., & Nicholas, L. J. (1995). Reducing suicide potential among high-risk youth. *Suicide & Life-Threatening Behavior*, 25, 276-296.

Hayes, L. M. (1983). And darkness closes in. *Criminal Justice & Behavior*, 10, 461-484.

Henry, J. A. (1989). A fatal toxicity index for antidepressant poisoning. *Acta Psychiatrica Scandinavica*, Supplement 354, 37-45.

Jordan, F. B., Schmeckpepper, K., & Strope, M. (1987). Jail suicides by hanging. *American Journal of Forensic Medicine & Pathology*, 8, 27-31.

Kalafat, J., & Elias, M. (1994). An evaluation of a school-based suicide awareness intervention. *Suicide & Life-Threatening Behavior*, 24, 224-233.

Korkeila, J., Salminen, J. K., Hiekkanen, H., & Salokangas, R. K. R. (2007). Use of antidepressants and suicide rate in Finland. *Journal of Clinical Psychiatry*, 68, 505-511.

Kreitman, N. (1976). The coal gas story. *British Journal of Preventive & Social Medicine*, 30, 86-93.

Kurdyak, P. A., Juurlink, D. N., & Mamdani, M. M. (2007). The effect of antidepressant warnings on prescribing trends in Ontario, Canada. *American Journal of Public Health*, 97, 750-754.

Lester, D. (1987). *Suicide as a learned behavior*. Springfield, IL: Charles Thomas.

Lester, D (1989). *Can we prevent suicide?* New York: AMS.

Lester, D. (1991). *Psychotherapy for suicidal clients*. Springfield, IL: Charles Thomas.

Lester, D. (1992). State initiatives in addressing youth suicide. *Social Psychiatry & Psychiatric Epidemiology*, 27, 75-77.

Lester, D. (1993). Controlling crime facilitators. *Crime Prevention Studies*, 1, 35-54.

Lester, D. (1994). Access to gambling opportunities and compulsive gambling. *International Journal of the Addictions*, 29, 1611-1616.

Lester, D. (1997). Evaluating the effectiveness of suicide prevention centers. *Suicide & Life-Threatening Behavior*, 27, 304-310.

Lester, D. (1998). Preventing suicide by restricting access to methods for suicide. *Archives of Suicide Research*, 4, 7-24.

Lester, D., & Abe, K. (1992). The effects of the switch from coal gas to natural gas on the accidental death rate. *Accident Analysis & Prevention*, 24, 157-160.

Lineberry, T. W., Bostwick, J. M., Beebe, T. J., & Decker, P. A. (2007). Impact of the FDA black box warning on physician antidepressant prescribing and practice patterns. *Mayo Clinic Proceedings*, 82, 516-522.

Ludwig, J., & Marcotte, D. E. (2005). Anti-depressants, suicide, and drug regulation. *Journal of Policy Analysis & Management*, 24, 249-272.

Mackesy-Amiti, M. E., Fendrich, M., Libby, S., Goldenberg, D., & Grossman, J. (1996). Assessment of knowledge gains in proactive training for postvention. *Suicide & Life-Threatening Behavior*, 26, 161-180.

Marshall, M. C. D. (1971). The indigenous nurse. *Seminars in Psychiatry*, 3, 264-270.

Milane, M. S., Suchard, M. A., Wong, M. L., & Licinio, J. (2006). Modeling of the temporal patterns of fluoxetine prescriptions and suicide rates in the United States. *PLOS Medicine*, 3(6).

Porter, K. K., & Jones, M. J. (1990). Wrist slashing in a detention center. *American Journal of Forensic Medicine & Pathology*, 11, 319-323.

Ratcliffe, R. W. (1962). The open door. *Lancet*, ii, 188-190.

Reinecke, M. A., & Didie, E. R. (2005). Cognitive-behavioral therapy with suicidal patients. In R. I. Yufit & D. Lester (Eds.) *Assessment, treatment, and prevention of suicidal behavior*, pp. 205-234. Hoboken, NJ: John Wiley.

Rutz, W., van Knorring, L., & Walinder, J. (1989). Frequency of suicide on Gotland after systematic postgraduate education of general practitioners. *Acta Psychiatrica Scandinavica*, 80, 151-154.

Ryerson, D. (1990). Suicide awareness education in schools. *Death Studies*, 14, 371-390.

Seiden, R. H. (1977). Suicide prevention. *Omega*, 8, 267-276.

Seiden, R. H., & Spence, M. (1983-1984). A tale of two bridges. *Omega*, 14, 201-209.

Shaffer, D., Garland, A., Gould, M., Fisher, P., & Trautman, P. (1988). Preventing teenage suicide. *Journal of the American Academy of Child & Adolescent Psychiatry*, 27, 675-687.

Shneidman, E. S. (1967). Description of the NIMH Center for Studies of Suicide Prevention. *Bulletin of Suicidology*, July, 2-7

Smith, D. I. (1988). Effectiveness of restrictions on availability as a means of reducing alcohol-related problems. *Contemporary Drug Problems*, 15, 627-684.

Soumerai, S. B., Avorn, J., Gortmaker, S., & Hawley, S. (1987). Effect of government and commercial warnings on reducing prescription misuse. *American Journal of Public Health*, 77, 1518.

Stack, S. (1990). Media impacts on suicide. In D. Lester (Ed.) *Current concepts of suicide*, pp. 107-120. Philadelphia: Charles Press.

Stengel, E. (1964). *Suicide and attempted suicide*. Baltimore: Penguin.

Stone, W. E. (1984). Means of the cause of death in Texas jail suicides. *American Jails*, 4(1), 50-53.

Swenson, D. D. (1968). First annual conference on suicidology. *Bulletin of Suicidology*, December, 46-48.

Van Praag, H. M. (2003). A stubborn behavior. *World Journal of Biological Psychiatry*, 4, 184-191.

Walk, D. (1967). Suicide and community care. *British Journal of Psychiatry*, 113, 1381-1391.

Wenckstern, S., & Leenaars, A. A. (1991). Suicide postvention. In A. A. Leenaars & S. Wenckstern (Eds.) *Suicide prevention in schools*, pp. 181-195. New York: Hemisphere.

Wortley, R. (2002). *Situational prison control*. Cambridge, UK: Cambridge University Press.

Zonda, T., & Lester, D. (2006-2007). Preventing suicide by educating general practitioners. *Omega*, 54, 53-57.

Chapter 2

DOMESTIC GAS

The strategy of preventing suicide by removing access (or restricting access) to lethal methods for suicide first came to prominence as a result of the detoxification of domestic gas in England. From the late 1950s on, the new manufacturing process for domestic gas changed its composition, and then, between 1968 and 1977, domestic gas was changed from coal gas (which has a high carbon monoxide content) to natural gas (which has no carbon monoxide). After 1977, suicide by means of domestic gas became much more difficult and, if it killed, it did so by suffocation rather than poisoning with carbon monoxide..

Hassall and Trethowan (1972) noted the decline in suicides using domestic gas in Birmingham, and Kreitman (1976) noted that the total English suicide rate declined by 40% between 1963 and 1975, parallel with the decline in the toxicity of domestic gas. The percentage of suicides using domestic gas declined from 49.8% in 1958 to 0.2% in 1977 (Clarke & Mayhew, 1988).

The decline in the overall suicide rate in England and Wales was found for men 45 years of age and older, whereas younger men seem to have switched to alternative methods for suicide. For women, the critical age was 25 years of age or older - women older than 25 did not seem to switch methods for suicide whereas the younger women did switch methods. Overall, Wells (1981) estimated that 6,700 lives had been saved by 1980.

This phenomenon was observed in many countries, including Australia (Burvill, 1990), Belgium (Moens et al., 1989) and Germany (Wiedermann and Weyerer, 1993).

Alternative explanations were proposed by those who doubted the connection between the detoxification of domestic gas and the reduction in the English suicide rate, including (1) changes in the classification of causes of death, (2) improved medical and ambulance services leading to more potential suicides being saved, (3) improved psychiatric and psychotherapeutic care, (4) the growth in the network of suicide prevention centers established by the Samaritans, and (5) improvements in the social and economic well-being of the population. Clarke and Mayhew (1988) argued that there was little evidence for these alternative explanations.

COMPARING DIFFERENT NATIONS

England and Wales, Scotland and the Netherlands

Clarke and Mayhew (1989) compared the impact on suicide of detoxifying domestic gas in England and Wales, Scotland and the Netherlands. In all three countries, the detoxification of domestic gas virtually eliminated domestic gas suicides. In England and Wales, the overall suicide rate declined 38% from 1963 to 1975; in Scotland the overall suicide rate declined slightly, about 7% from 1962 to 1975; while in the Netherlands, the overall suicide rate remained roughly constant from 1963 to 1968 and then rose thereafter.

Clarke and Mayhew noted that the use of domestic gas for suicide was much less common in the Netherlands than in England and Wales. For example, the accidental death rate in 1956-1959 due to domestic gas (a measure of the availability of domestic gas in homes) was only 0.54 per 100,000 per year in the Netherlands as compared to 1.83 in England and Wales and 2.00 in Scotland. Indeed, only about 59% of Dutch homes received domestic gas as compared to 75% of homes in England and Wales and 66% of homes in Scotland.

In Great Britain, Kreitman and Platt (1984) reported that, as domestic gas was detoxified from 1964 to 1972, the association between unemployment and the suicide rate by methods other than domestic gas was positive, a common finding in time-series studies of nations. However, the association between unemployment and the overall suicide rate was negative, because, according to Kreitman and Platt, of the virtual elimination of suicide by domestic gas. After 1972, the association with unemployment was positive both for the overall suicide rate and for the suicide rate by all methods other than domestic gas.

Lester (1991) replicated the study by Clarke and Mayhew in the Netherlands using inferential statistics (rather than a simple presentation of figures). He found that the detoxification of domestic gas from 1958 to 1975 was accompanied by a decrease in the suicide rate by domestic gas from 1.93 per 100,000 per year to

0.18. There was, however, an increase in the suicide rate by other methods over the same period, from 5.57 to 9.70. Thus, substitution of methods for suicide seems to have occurred.

In Scotland from 1960 (when the percentage of carbon monoxide in domestic gas was 11.1%) to 1975 (when the percentage was 0.7%), Lester and Hodgson (1992) found that, as domestic gas was detoxified, the suicide rate using domestic gas declined from 3.86 to 0.21, while the suicide rate using all other methods continued to rise at the same pace as before detoxification (from 4.02 to 7.95). The total suicide rate, however, stopped increasing and held steady (7.88 in 1960 and 8.16 in 1975).

As we will see later in Chapter 3, the use of car exhaust for suicide in England Wales rose rapidly during the period of the detoxification of domestic gas, in line with the increase in ownership of cars which had no emission controls and, therefore, highly toxic exhaust gas. These two methods are very similar and so, if one is made less available, the other may become relatively more attractive. Despite the switching of methods by men, there was a lag in the displacement, and so many lives might have been saved in the interim period.

All of the studies reviewed in this section were time-series studies. In an ecological study (i.e., a study of a set of regions during one time period), Sainsbury (1986) looked at 10 English cities and claimed that detoxification of domestic gas had no impact on the suicide rate from 1958 to 1967. Lester (1990c) looked at these regional effects in England statistically, comparing the impact of the detoxification of domestic gas and the presence of a suicide prevention center on suicides rates from 1958 to 1967 (the same period as used by Sainsbury). This regional study found no significant impact on the suicide rate from either factor, but the sample sizes were small, and the cities with less toxic gas at the end of the study period still had high levels of carbon monoxide in their domestic gas supply (about 5%).

Northern Ireland

Curran and Lester (1991) found that the detoxification of domestic gas in Northern Ireland was not accompanied by an increase in the rate of suicide using other methods. From 1964 to 1973, the suicide rate using domestic gas dropped from 2.06 to 0.39, while the suicide rate by all other methods rose only from 3.16 to 4.18. However, both rates peaked in 1966-1968 at 1.55 and 5.73, so that both suicide rates declined after the late 1960s. Substitution of method did not, therefore, appear to occur. These data indicate clearly that the choice of the time period studied can markedly affect the conclusions.

The United States

In the United States, the switch from coal gas to natural gas for domestic supplies occurred much earlier than in Europe. Date are available only from 1946 on, at which point in time 45% of homes were already using natural (non-toxic) gas. By 1970, 99% of homes were using natural gas.

Lester (1990a) found that the suicide rate using domestic gas declined from 0.93 per 100,000 per year in 1946 to 0.02 in 1970. The overall suicide rate, however, remained roughly constant, changing from 11.48 in 1946 to 11.45 in 1970, although declining in the 1950s (to as low as 9.67 in 1957).

Lester noted that the decline in the use of domestic gas for suicide by men was paralleled by an increase in the use of car exhaust for suicide The suicide rate by car exhaust rose from 1.09 in 1950 to 1.48 in 1970, but the suicide rate using any gas still declined (from 1.94 in 1950 to 1.51 in 1970). The suicide rate by all non-gas methods changed from 15.75 in 1950 to 15.30 in 1970. So, some men may have switched to car exhaust, but substitution of method once domestic gas was detoxified was not complete.

For women, on the other hand, there was not as large as displacement to car exhaust over the period. Suicide rates by women using any form of gas declined from 0.73 in 1950 to 0.62 in 1970, but the suicide rate by all non-gas methods rose from 4.32 in 1950 to 5.95 in 1970. Apparently, this was a period of rising suicide rates in women in the United States.

Using the accidental death rate from a method as an index of its availability, Lester (1990b) found that the accidental and suicidal death rates from all types of gases in the United States were positively associated for the period 1950-1984. Thus, the more gas was available, the greater its use for suicide.

Japan

Lester and Abe (1989) studied the impact of the detoxification of domestic gas in Japan on the suicide rate from 1969 to 1982. They found, first of all, that the suicide rate using domestic gas and the production of toxic gas showed a similar trend (see also, Yamasawa et al., 1980). Both increased until the early 1970s, whereupon both showed a dramatic decrease. However, Lester and Abe noted that the suicide rate by all other methods increased, but less so during the latter part of the period. The slope of the regression line for 1969-1975 was 455 and for 1975-1982 only 114. So displacement to other methods of suicide slowed down during this period.

Lester and Abe (1990) also reported that the accidental and suicide rates from domestic gas were positively associated for the period 1950-1980, supporting the hypothesis that the availability of toxic domestic gas (as measured by the accidental death rate from domestic gas) was associated with the suicide rate using domestic gas.

Switzerland

Lester (1990d) found that, as domestic gas was detoxified in Switzerland from 1951 to 1968, not only did the suicide rate using domestic gas decline (from 3.76 to 0.50 for men and from 4.00 to 0.29 for women), but so did the overall suicide rate (from 30.98 to 25.03 for men and from 11.64 to 9.52 for women), indicating that people did not switch methods for suicide once domestic gas became less toxic.

A COMPARISON OF CHANGES IN SIX NATIONS

Lester (1995) compared the changes in suicide rates by domestic gas, by all other methods and overall in six nations: Japan, the Netherlands, Northern Ireland, Scotland, Switzerland and the United States. Lester did not report the exact data in his published report, but the unpublished data are shown here in Table 2.1.

In three nations (Northern Ireland, Scotland and Switzerland), the suicide rate using domestic gas was high initially, and in all of them the overall suicide rate declined as domestic gas was detoxified.

In three nations (Japan, the Netherlands and the United States), the suicide rate using domestic gas was low initially, and in all of them the overall suicide rate increased as domestic gas was detoxified.

Thus, the total suicide rate appears to have been reduced by making toxic domestic gas less available only in those nations where it was a common method for suicide.

Table 2.1. Changes in suicide rates in
six nations as domestic gas was detoxified

Suicide Rates per 100,000 per year		By Domestic Gas	By All Other Methods	Total
Japan	1969	1.12	13.43	14.55
	1982	0.65	16.86	17.51
	Change			+2.96
The Netherlands	1958	1.93	5.57	7.50
	1975	0.18	9.70	9.88
	Change			+2.38
Northern Ireland	1964	2.06	3.36	5.42
	1973	0.39	4.18	4.57
	Change			-0.85
Scotland	1962	4.21	4.89	9.10
	1975	0.21	7.95	8.16
	Change			-0.94
Switzerland	1954	3.58	18.73	22.31
	1968	0.39	16.76	17.16
	Change			-5.15
United States	1950	0.73	10.53	11.26
	1970	0.02	11.43	11.45
	Change			+0.19

Unpublished data from Lester.

DISCUSSION

This review has highlighted a very difficult problem in analyzing the impact of making a lethal method for suicide (in the present chapter, domestic gas) less available. Many changes occur in a society, and it is very difficult to examine the impact of one change while ignoring the other changes. This is illustrated by a study reported by Nordentoft et al. (2007) who examined the changing suicide rate in Denmark from 1970 to 2000. The availability of toxic coal gas declined steadily after 1980, and additional measures were instituted such as automatic closure of the gas supply if the gas is not lit and reduced use of gas ovens. The use of domestic gas as a method for suicide declined steadily throughout the period and was not used at all after 1994. However many other changes occurred during the same period, such as a decreased availability of common medications such as barbiturates and dextropropoxyphene, and the increased use of catalytic converters which reduced the toxicity of car exhaust. The steady decline in the total suicide rate in Denmark since 1980 could be a result of all of these changes, as well as changes in social conditions such as the unemployment rate, the divorce rate and alcohol consumption.

Burvill (1990) noted in Australia that, as the use of domestic gas for suicide declined, the suicide rate by all gases, after staying steady (for men) or showing a slight decrease (for women), began to rise in the mid-1980s as people switched to car exhaust. For example, the percentage of male suicides using domestic gas declined from 7% in 1951 to ½% in the mid-1980s; for car exhaust the percentage increased from 2½% in 1951 to 22% in the mid-1980s. For women, the use of domestic gas declined from 19% to ½% while the use of car exhaust increased from ½% to 13%. In Germany, people seemed to have switched to the use of poisons rather than car exhaust (Wiedermann and Weyerer, 1993).

The conclusion from the studies reviewed in this chapter is that a change in the availability of one method for suicide, in this case domestic gas, reduces its use for suicide but it has an impact on the overall suicide rate only when that method was a common method for suicide initially.

REFERENCES

Burvill, P. W. (1990). The changing pattern of suicide by gassing in Australia, 1910-1987. *Acta Psychiatrica Scandinavica*, 81, 178-184.

Clarke, R. V., & Mayhew, P. (1988). The British gas suicide story and its criminological implications. In. M. Tonry & N. Morris (Eds.) *Crime & Justice*, 10, 79-116.

Clarke, R. V., & Mayhew, P. (1989). Crime as opportunity. *British Journal of Criminology*, 29, 35-46.

Curran, P. S., & Lester, D. (1991). Trends in the methods used for suicide in Northern Ireland. *Ulster Medical Journal*, 60, 58-62.

Hassall, C., & Trethowan, W. M. (1972). Suicide in Birmingham. *British Medical Journal*, March 18, 717-718.

Kreitman, N. (1976). The coal gas story. *British Journal of Preventive & Social Medicine*, 30, 86-93.

Kreitman, N., & Platt, S. (1984). Suicide, unemployment, and domestic gas dextoxification in Britain. *Journal of Epidemiology & Community Health*, 38, 1-6.

Lester, D. (1990a). The effects of detoxification of domestic gas on suicide in the United States. *American Journal of Public Health*, 80, 80-81.

Lester, D. (1990b). Accidental death rates and suicide. *Activitas Nervosa Superior*, 32, 130-131.

Lester, D. (1990c). Was gas detoxification or the establishment of suicide prevention centers responsible for the decline in the British suicide rate? *Psychological Reports*, 66, 286.

Lester, D. (1990d). The effect of the detoxification of domestic gas in Switzerland on the suicide rate. *Acta Psychiatrica Scandinavica*, 82, 383-384.

Lester, D. (1991). Effects of detoxification of domestic gas on suicide in the Netherlands. *Psychological Reports*, 68, 202.

Lester, D. (1995). Effects of the detoxification of domestic gas on suicide rates in six nations. *Psychological Reports*, 77, 294.

Lester, D., & Abe, K. (1989). The effect of restricting access to lethal methods for suicide. *Acta Psychiatrica Scandinavica*, 80, 180-182.

Lester, D., & Abe, K. (1990). The availability of lethal methods for suicide and the suicide rate. *Stress Medicine*, 6, 275-276.

Lester, D., & Hodgson, J. (1992). The effects of the detoxification of domestic gas on the suicide rate in Scotland. *European Journal of Psychiatry*, 6, 171-174.

Moens, G. F., Loysch, M. J., Honggokoesoemo, S., & van de Voorde, H. (1989). Recent trends in methods of suicide. *Acta Psychiatrica Scandinavica*, 79, 207-215.

Nordentoft, M., Qin, P., Helweg-Larsen, K., & Juel, K. (2007). Restrictions in means for suicide. *Suicide & Life-Threatening Behavior*, 37, 688-697.

Sainsbury, P. (1986). The epidemiology of suicide. In A. Roy (Ed.) *Suicide*, pp. 17-40. Baltimore: Williams & Wilkins.

Wells, N. (1981). *Suicide and deliberate self-harm*. London, UK: Office of Health Economics.

Wiedermann, A., & Weyerer, S. (1993). The impact of availability, attraction and lethality of suicide methods on suicide rates in Germany. *Acta Psychiatrica Scandinavica*, 88, 364-368.

Yamasawa, K., Nishimukai, H., Ohbora, Y., & Inoue, K. (1980). A statistical study of suicide through intoxication. *Acta Medicinae Legalis et Socialis*, 30, 187-192.

Chapter 3

CAR EXHAUST

After 14 minutes—Respiration can be done only by mouth.

After 15 minutes—Water is pouring out from the hose.

After 16 minutes—Goodbye, Mum and Papa! Mr. and Miss. So and So (six persons' names).

After 17 minutes—Still, I am living. It is asthmatic respiration. Now, I will sleep.

— From the suicide note of a car-exhaust suicide
(from Tsunenari et al., 1985)

Suicide by car exhaust became much more frequent toward the end of the twentieth century. In some countries, dramatic increases in the use of car exhaust for suicide were reported. The use of car exhaust rose, for example, in England and Wales in the 1980s, and Lindesay (1991) noted that this increase was especially noticeable in the elderly for whom the rate rose from 0.5 per 100,000 in 1965 to almost 2.5 in 1986.[1]

Several studies have looked at the characteristics of those who use this method for suicide. Ostrom, Thorson and Eriksson (1996) in Sweden found that the use of car exhaust for suicide was more common in rural areas and in men. Most of these suicides used a car in the open air and a vacuum-cleaner tube to pass the car exhaust into the car. In Denmark, Theilade (1990) found that the use of car exhaust for suicide was less common than domestic gas. More of the car-exhaust suicides took place outside (rather than in a garage), and those suicides

---

[1] Suicide using the exhaust from motorbikes is also possible (e.g., Martinez & Ballesteros, 2006).

outside were younger than those in garages. Car-exhaust suicides differed in age and sex from domestic gas suicides, being younger and more often male.

In the Lothian and Borders region of Scotland, Busuttil et al. (1994) found that the car-exhaust suicide rate rose after 1990 and was more common in men, those aged 35-44, those living in rural areas, and in Spring and Summer. The location varied by season, with an outdoor location more common in Summer. In Australia, Routley (1994) found that the most popular location for car-exhaust suicide was in the suicide's own home - in the garden or garage.

De Leo et al. (2002) compared the characteristics of men using non-domestic gas (mostly car exhaust) with those using hanging and firearms for suicide in Queensland, Australia. Those using car exhaust more often lived alone, left a suicide note and (along with those using hanging) had made previous attempts at suicide. Those using car exhaust less often were in legal trouble or had a psychotic disorder. They did not differ in the presence of a history of depression or previous psychiatric treatment.

RESEARCH ON REDUCING THE TOXICITY OF CAR EXHAUST

The concentration of toxic and lethal carbon monoxide in car exhaust has been reduced in recent years, mainly as a result of catalytic converters added to cars in an effort to reduce environmental pollution. The result has been that it has become more difficult to commit suicide using car exhaust. The time to die has been lengthened by the reduction in carbon monoxide content, making it more feasible for potential suicides to change their mind, since death from simple suffocation (from the displacement of oxygen) takes much longer than poisoning by carbon monoxide, and it is more likely that passers-by will intervene.[1] Studies on the impact on emission controls for car exhaust on suicide rates has been carried out in five countries: Australia, Japan, Northern Ireland, the United States of America and the United Kingdom.

---

[1] Death is still possible from asphyxiation as a result of depletion of oxygen inside the car due to breathing and displacement by the car exhaust (Schmunk & Kaplan, 2002; deRoux, 2006). Vossberg and Skolnick (1999) reported a case of a man who breathed car exhaust from a car with a catalytic converter for 8 to 10 hours in a closed garage and who survived.

Australia

Emission controls for car-exhaust emissions were introduced in Australia in 1986. Routley and Ozanne-Smith (1998) looked at the effect of these regulations on suicide by car exhaust from 1970–1995. During this period, the registrations of cars per capita increased, as did the suicide rate using car exhaust, although the suicide rate using car exhaust may have reached a plateau after 1990. In addition, the number of attempted suicides using car exhaust increased. Brennan et al. (2006) confirmed that the emission controls had little effect on suicide rates using car exhaust. However, they did note that, in 2002, only 9% of car-exhaust suicides used newer cars with emission controls whereas these cars constituted 26% of cars in the province. It is to be expected, therefore, that, as older cars with no emissions controls are taken out of use, then the use of car exhaust for suicide might decline.

These results are puzzling. The increase in suicides using car exhaust after 1986 did not fit with expectations. However, the increasing number of survivors from attempts at suicide using car exhaust does suggest that car exhaust was less toxic and less lethal, and so potential suicides were saved.

Routley and Ozanne-Smith looked at 100 cases of car-exhaust suicides in 1994–1996, and found that 36 percent of them used cars built after 1986 and, therefore, equipped with the new emission controls. The mean blood levels of carboxyhemoglobin were similar in the suicides using the old and the new cars.

Routley and Ozanne-Smith suggested several reasons why car-exhaust suicides had not declined. (1) Carbon monoxide emissions while a car is idling had not been measured for the new cars and could be higher than the levels measured when driving. (2) Carbon monoxide emissions have not been measured inside cars, whose cabins vary in volume, when the car exhaust enters through a hose connected to the exhaust pipe. (3) Carbon monoxide content may be higher before the engine warms up. (4) Catalytic converters deteriorate over time.

Japan

Lester and Abe (1989) examined the effects of the increasing ownership of cars in Japan on the suicide rate using car exhaust. Suicide by car exhaust rose from less than 0.02 per 100,000 per year in 1965 to 1.33 in 1982. Meanwhile suicide by all other methods rose from about 14.7 in 1965 to 16.2 in 1982. Thus, the proportion of suicides using car exhaust rose dramatically during the period, from 0.1% to 7.6%. The ownership of cars increased almost linearly from 1965 to

1982 and, along with this change, the suicide rate using car exhaust rose dramatically, with an especially steep increase from 1973 to 1975. After (weak) emission controls were introduced in 1975, the increase in the suicide rate by car exhaust lessened noticeably but did not decline. The suicide rate by all other methods, however, stayed relatively constant over this period. Because the emission controls were weak, car exhaust was still capable of killing. Nonetheless, the results appeared to indicate that the tightening of emission controls on car exhaust may have inhibited its *increasing* use for suicide.

In their study, Lester and Abe noted that the suicide rate by all other methods rose up to 1973, along with the increasing suicide rate by car exhaust. This period, therefore, shows little evidence of switching. As suicide by car exhaust became more common, so did suicide by all other methods.

Northern Ireland

In Northern Ireland, Curran and Lester (1991) found that, as suicide using car exhaust become more common, suicide by all other methods did not become less common.

The United States

In the United States, the 1970 Clean Air Act set standards for car-exhaust emissions, and catalytic converters were introduced nationwide in 1975 (although some states, such as California, had required them earlier). The result was that the carbon monoxide content in car exhaust dropped from 8.5% to 0.05% by 1980. Mott et al. (2002) looked at trends in deaths from car-exhaust in the United States from 1968 to 1998 and documented that the suicide rate using car exhaust had declined significantly over each ten-year period (1968-1978, 1979-1988 and 1989-1998).[1] The decline was significant for both men and women and for all age groups.

Marzuk et al. (1992) compared suicide rates by each method in the five counties of New York City in 1984-1987. For methods with equal access across the counties, such as hanging and cutting/piercing, there were no differences in

---

[1] During the 30-year period, 60,868 suicidal deaths from car exhaust were officially recorded, as well as 2,056 deaths of undetermined intent (and, in addition, 12,811 suicides and 5,011 deaths of undetermined intent from carbon monoxide of undetermined mechanism).

suicide rates. The two counties with the most garages in private residences (Queens and Staten Island) had much higher suicide rates by car exhaust than the other three counties. (The five counties also differed in suicide rates by jumping, prescribed medications, trains and subways, methods for which the availability also differed by county.)

Lester and Frank (1989) found that the number of cars per capita in the states in 1980 was positively associated with the use of car exhaust for suicide, but not with the suicide rate by all other methods or with the total suicide rate. (This suggests that switching methods did not occur.) Incidentally, they found that a greater proportion of female suicides used car exhaust versus males suicides (9.9% versus 6.7%), whites versus nonwhites (7.9% versus 1.8%), and in the winter versus the summer (7.9% versus 6.0%).

Lester (1989b) looked at the trends over time by sex more closely. He found that, after emission controls were introduced, men showed an immediate decrease in the use of car exhaust for suicide. Women, on the other hand, did not show a decrease in the use of car exhaust for suicide until 1975, suggesting that the implications of the arrival of emission controls for car exhaust was not immediately apparent to women. As more attempted suicides using car exhaust survived (e.g., Landers, 1981; Hays & Bornstein, 1984), and the press reported this, females may have become more aware of the increased difficulty of committing suicide using car exhaust.

Lester (1989a) looked at suicide rates by car exhaust over time from 1950-1984 in the United States, using the toxicity index developed by Clarke and Lester. He found that a simple measure of cars per capita was associated with the female car-exhaust suicide rate and the percentage of female suicides using car-exhaust for suicide, but these associations for men did not differ significantly from zero. In contrast, the toxicity index of the cars was related to the male car-exhaust suicide rate and the percentage of male suicides using car-exhaust for suicide, but these associations for women did not differ significantly from zero.

It has been suggested that the availability of a method for suicide can be assessed by looking at the accidental mortality rate from that method. Lester (1993) found that the accidental death rate from car exhaust was positively associated over the states of America with the suicide rate from car exhaust.

Lester (1990b) reported that the accidental death rate from car exhaust was positively associated over time in the United States with the suicide rate from car exhaust for the period 1950–1984, and Lester and Abe (1990) replicated this result in Japan for the period 1950–1980. However, in a multiple regression analysis, Lester (1995) found that the suicide rate by car exhaust in this period was not predicted by the accidental death rate from car exhaust or the number of cars per capita. The percentage of suicides using car exhaust was predicted by the number of cars per capita (but not by the accidental death rate from car exhaust).

Shelef (1994) calculated the number of suicides using car exhaust that actually occurred in the United States for the period 1970–1987 and the number that would be expected given the growth in population and car ownership if no emission controls had been introduced. The savings in life over the 18 year period came to 16,911. If some of these would *not* have switched methods for suicide, then those lives were saved.

The United Kingdom

Clarke and Lester (1987; Lester & Clarke, 1988) compared suicide using car exhaust in the United States, where emissions controls had been introduced, with the United Kingdom where they had not. Rates of suicide using car exhaust declined somewhat after the introduction of emission controls in the United States, whereas the suicide rate using car exhaust rose consistently through the 1970s and 1980s in the United Kingdom. (It must be remembered that older, more toxic cars were still in use and that emission controls can be disconnected to permit gas richer in carbon monoxide to fill the car or garage.)

The decrease in car-exhaust suicide in the United States was not as great as the reduction in toxic car exhaust would have predicted, but the rate did decrease. In contrast, in the United Kingdom, the car-exhaust suicide rate rose dramatically faster than the increase in car ownership would have predicted. Clarke and Lester suggested that this dramatic increase could have resulted from four possibilities: (1) increasing awareness of the possibility of suicide by car exhaust as the press reported such suicides, (2) an increase in the sale of hatchback cars which make it easier to place a hose from the exhaust pipe into the car interior, (3) an increase in the building of garages for cars, making car-exhaust suicide more feasible without discovery by passers-by, and (4) the detoxification of domestic gas (switching from toxic coal gas to less toxic natural gas) may have forced those wishing to use gas for suicide to switch to an alternative gas.

Clarke and Lester noted that, since car exhaust was not a common method for suicide in either country, detecting possible displacement (switching to other methods for suicide) was difficult. Clarke and Lester also noted that car exhaust was a more popular method for suicide in the United States than in the United Kingdom, possibly because of the greater per capita car ownership of cars in America and the greater salience of the car in the cultural consciousness of Americans.

Kendell (1998) looked at suicides from car exhaust in Scotland from 1990–1997 and noted that the number of car-exhaust suicides had decreased. A similar trend was noted for England and Wales. More recently, Amos, Appleby and Kiernan (2001) looked at the impact of legislation regarding catalytic converters implemented in 1993 in England and Wales. They noted a significant decrease in the percentage of cars without catalytic converters and corresponding decreases in the number of car-exhaust suicides, the percentage of suicides using car exhaust and the suicide rate using car exhaust. During the same time period (1992–1998), the total suicide rate also decreased, despite the fact that the suicide rate by hanging increased. (The suicide rate by all other methods other than hanging and car exhaust did not, however, increase.) The apparent substitution of hanging for car exhaust for suicide was most pronounced in men aged 15–44[1] for whom the total suicide rate increased from 1992 to 1998. For all other sex-by-age groups, the overall suicide rate decreased.

Wilson and Saunders (2000) examined the impact in the UK of the increasing use of diesel engines which also reduce the level of carbon monoxide in car exhaust over that from gasoline engines. They found no impact from this change on the suicide rate using car exhaust prior to the introduction of catalytic converters.

CROSS-NATIONAL STUDIES

Lester (1994) examined the association between car ownership per capita and the suicide rates by method in a sample of 28 nations with available data. The association with suicide by "other gases" (meaning gases other than domestic gas and which is mainly car exhaust) was positive (and significantly different from zero) and with all other methods for suicide not significantly different from zero. Thus, nations with more cars per capita had higher suicide rates by car exhaust but not higher or lower rates by all other methods. This suggests that cars create suicides.

---

[1] Unlike previous observations on this phenomenon in England, Amos et al. took into account the disguising of suicides in the United Kingdom by coroners who classify them as "undetermined."

A Suicide "Hot Spot"

King and Frost (2005) noted that the car parks for the New Forest in New Hampshire, England, had become a popular venue for car-exhaust suicide, with an average of 10.0 each year. In 1998, a sign was erected in 26 of the 140 car parks advertising the Samaritans suicide prevention hotline. The Forestry Commission prohibited signs being erected in all car parks, apparently giving higher weight to the "beauty" of the car parks over the value of a human life. For the three years after the erection of these signs, the number of suicides each year in all of the car parks dropped from 9.0 to 3.3 each year, whereas the number of suicides elsewhere in the New Forest rose by 1.8 per year (from 13.5 to 15.3). The decrease of car-exhaust suicides in the car parks was found both for local residents and non-local visitors. It should be noted that the New Forest is the only suicide venue ever reported for car-exhaust suicide.

DISCUSSION

It is clear that suicide rate using car exhaust rises in countries as the per-capita car ownership increases. It is less clear that the imposition of emission controls for car exhaust reduces the use of car exhaust for suicide, both in terms of the suicide rate using car exhaust and the percentage of suicides using car exhaust. A reduction has been noted in some countries, such as the United States, but not in others such as Australia (see Table 3.1). It is also unclear whether there is a substitution effect, that is, displacement to other methods of suicide, and whether the substitution prevents a reduction in the overall suicide rate.

Car exhaust has never been a common method for suicide. For example, the rate of suicide by "other gasses" (that is, other than domestic gas) in 1960-1964 for some of the countries discussed in this chapter was: 0.9 per 100,000 per year for Australia, 0.3 for England and Wales, 0.0 in Japan and 1.1 in the United States (Lester, 1990a). The total suicide rates in these countries for the same period were 13.4, 11.7, 18.0 and 10.7, respectively. Car-exhaust suicides accounted for roughly 7%, 3%, 0% and 10% of the suicides in these countries. Therefore, changes in the toxicity of car exhaust would be unlikely to have a large impact on the overall suicide rate in these countries, especially since, during these periods, the availability of other methods of suicide (such as medications and firearms) was changing, as well as the social and economic conditions which have been shown to be associated with suicide rates.

Table 3.1. Impact of car ownership and emission controls on the suicide rate using car exhaust over time

	Impact of Emission Controls	Impact of Increase in Car Ownership	Impact of Increase in Diesal Engines
Australia	no	yes	—
Japan	no	yes	—
Scotland	yes	—	—
UK	—	yes	no
USA	yes	—	—

SOLUTIONS

Routley (1998) proposed some simple and inexpensive changes to cars that would make it more difficult to use car exhaust for suicide. First, she proposed changing the shape of the exhaust pipe (for example, by flattening out the opening) to make it more difficult to attached a hose pipe to the exhaust pipe. The cost of this was estimated to be about two Australian dollars per car.

Second, she proposed installing carbon monoxide detectors inside the compartment of the car which would sound an alarm and switch off the engine when the carbon monoxide concentration reached a predetermined level. The cost of this was estimated to be 130 Australian dollars per car.

A third, less effective, alternative is to install a device that would automatically turn off an idling engine after a predetermined time. This would require a potential suicide to keep turning the engine back on. These simple modifications would probably decrease the use of car exhaust for suicide.

REFERENCES

Amos, T., Appleby, L., & Kiernan, K. (2001). Changes in rates of suicide by car exhaust asphyxiation in England and Wales. *Psychological Medicine*, 31, 935-939.

Brennan, C., Routley, V., & Ozanne-Smith, J. (2006). Motor vehicle exhaust gas suicide in Victoria, Australia 1998-2002. *Crisis*, 27, 119-124.

Busuttil, A., Obafunwa, J. O., & Ahmed, A. (1994). Suicidal inhalation of vehicular exhaust in the Lothian and Borders Region of Scotland. *Human & Experimental Toxicology*, 13, 545-550.

Clarke, R. V., & Lester, D. (1987). Toxicity of car exhausts and opportunity for suicide. *Journal of Epidemiology & Community Health*, 41, 114-120.

Curran, P. S., & Lester, D. (1991). Trends in the methods used for suicide in Northern Ireland. *Ulster Medical Journal*, 60, 58-62.

De Leo, D., Evans, R., & Neulinger, K. (2002). Hanging, firearm, and non-domestic gas suicides among males. *Australian & New Zealand Journal of Psychiatry*, 36, 183-189.

deRoux, S. J. (2006). Suicidal asphyxiation by inhalation of automobile emission without carbon monoxide poisoning. *Journal of Forensic Sciences*, 51, 1158-1159.

Hays, P., & Bornstein, R. (1984). Failed suicide attempt by emission gas poisoning. *American Journal of Psychiatry*, 141, 592-593.

Kendell, R. E. (1998). Catalytic converters and prevention of suicides. *Lancet*, 352, 1525.

King, E., & Frost, N. (2005). The New Forest suicide prevention initiative (NFSPI). *Crisis*, 26, 25-33.

Landers, D. (1981). Unsuccessful suicide by carbon monoxide. *Western Journal of Medicine*, 135, 369-363.

Lester, D. (1989a). Suicide by car exhaust. *Perceptual & Motor Skills*, 68, 442.

Lester, D. (1989b). Changing rates of suicide by car exhaust in men and women in the United States after car exhaust was detoxified. *Crisis*, 10, 164-168.

Lester, D. (1990a). Changes in the method used for suicide in 16 countries from 1960 to 1980. *Acta Psychiatrica Scandinavica*, 81, 260-261.

Lester, D. (1990b). Accidental death rates and suicide. *Activitas Nervosa Superior*, 32, 130-131.

Lester, D (1993). Availability of methods for suicide and suicide rates. *Perceptual & Motor Skills*, 76, 1358.

Lester, D. (1994). Car ownership and suicide by car exhaust in nations of the world. *Perceptual & Motor Skills*, 79, 898.

Lester, D. (1995). The toxicity of car exhaust and its use as a method for suicide. *Psychological Reports*, 77, 1090.

Lester, D., & Abe, K. (1989). Car availability, exhaust toxicity, and suicide. *Annals of Clinical Psychiatry*, 1, 247-250.

Lester, D., & Abe, K. (1990). The availability of lethal methods for suicide and the suicide rate. *Stress Medicine*, 6, 275-276.

Lester, D., & Clarke, R. V. (1988). Effect of reduced toxicity of car exhaust. *American Journal of Public Health*, 78, 594.

Lester, D., & Frank, M. L. (1989). The use of motor vehicle exhaust for suicide and the availability of cars. *Acta Psychiatrica Scandinavica*, 79, 238-240.

Lindesay, J. (1991). Suicide in the elderly. *International Journal of Geriatric Psychiatry*, 6, 355-361.

Marzuk, P. M., Leon, A. C., Tardiff, K., Morgan, E. B., Stajic, M., & Mann, J. J. (1992). The effect of access to lethal methods of injury on suicide rates. *Archives of General Psychiatry*, 49, 451-458.

Martinez, M. A., & Ballesteros, S. (2006). Suicidal inhalation of motorbike exhaust. *Journal of Analytical Toxicology*, 30, 697-702.

Mott, J. A., Wolfe, M. I., Alverson, C. J., Macdonald, S. C., Bailey, C. R., Ball, L. B., Moorman, J. E., Somers, J. H., Mannino, D. M., & Redd, S. C. (2002). National vehicle emissions policies and practices and declining US carbon monoxide-related mortality. *Journal of the American Medical Association*, 288, 988-995.

Ohberg, A., Lonnqvist, J., Sarna, S., Vuori, E., & Penttila, A. Trends and availability of suicide methods in Finland. *British Journal of Psychiatry*, 1995, 166, 35-43.

Ostrom, M., Thorson, J., & Eriksson, A. (1996). Carbon monoxide suicide from car exhausts. *Social Science & Medicine*, 42, 447-451.

Routley, V. (1988). *Motor vehicle exhaust gassing suicides in Australia*. Clayton, Australia: Monash University, Accident Research Center.

Routley, V. (1994). Non-traffic motor vehicle related injuries. *Hazard*, (September, #20), 1-9.

Routley, V. H., & Ozanne-Smith, J. (1998). The impact of catalytic converters on motor vehicle exhaust gas suicides. *Medical Journal of Australia*, 168, 65-67.

Schmunk, G. A., & Kaplan, J. A. (2002). Asphyxial deaths caused by automobile. *American Journal of Forensic Medicine & Pathology*, 23, 123-126

Shelef, M. (1994). Unanticipated benefits of automotive emission control. *Science of the Total Environment*, 146/147, 93-101.

Thielade, P. (1990). Carbon monoxide poisoning. *American Journal of Forensic Medicine & Pathology*, 11, 219-225.

Tsunenari, S., Kanda, M., Yonemitsu, K., & Yoshida, S. (1985). Suicidal carbon monoxide inhalation of exhaust fumes. *American Journal of Forensic Medicine & Pathology*, 6, 233-239.

Vossberg, B., & Skolnick, J. (1999). The role of catalytic converters in automobile carbon monoxide poisoning. *Chest*, 115, 580-581.

Wilson, R. C., & Saunders, P. J. (2000). The impact of legislation and changing vehicle propulsion methods on suicides using motor vehicle exhaust gases across the UK. *Journal of Epidemiology & Community Health, 54,* 797.

Chapter 4

JUMPING

It was the Golden Gate Bridge or nothing. I believed it was the way

I was attracted to the bridge—an affinity between me, the Golden Gate Bridge and death—there is a kind of form to it, a certain grace and beauty.

— Rosen, 1975, p. 290

These two quotes are from people who jumped from the Golden Gate Bridge but survived. They illustrate the lure of publicized suicide venues.

Some of the most well-known suicide venues in the world are places from which to jump, and it seems obvious that one way of preventing these suicides would be to fence in such places. For example, between 1931 and 1947, sixteen people committed suicide from the Empire State Building in Manhattan (Ellis & Allen, 1961), and the observation deck at the top was eventually enclosed in order to prevent suicides. It is surprising how difficult it has been to implement this simple tactic for preventing suicides at other venues.

The goals of this chapter are:

(1) to present some basic facts about suicide by jumping (who commits suicide by this method?) and related to this,

(2) is it true that this method is favored by those who are psychiatrically ill and what are the implications of this for suicide prevention, and finally

(3) what has been the impact of fencing in the places from which people jump? Does it prevent suicides by jumping and, furthermore, does it reduce the suicide rate?

First let us look at the places from which people jump.

SUICIDE VENUES

Suicide by jumping from high bridges appears from newspaper reports to be a common way of committing suicide, and there are some bridges that are well-known as suicide venues such as the Golden Gate Bridge in San Francisco, California.

Cliffs, volcanoes and other structures have also become suicide venues, inclduing the cliffs at Beachy Head in England (Surtees, 1982), the Eiffel Tower in France (Derobert et al., 1965), and Mt Mihara in Japan (Simpson, 1978). Jumping into the water above a water fall and going over the falls can also result in a famous suicide venue, such as Niagara Falls between Canada and America (Lester & Brockopp, 1971; Ross & Lester, 1991). People also jump to their deaths from high-rise apartments buildings (Lester, 1994) and high-rise hotels and casinos (Hanzlick et al., 1990; Lester & Jason, 1989).

Seiden and Spence (1982, 1983-1984) compared suicides from two similar bridges in the San Francisco area: the Golden Gate Bridge and the Bay Bridge. Both bridges opened in the 1930s (1937 and 1936, respectively), and they are of similar height above the water (200 feet). The Golden Gate Bridge carries about half the traffic of the Bay Bridge, is only $1/8^{th}$ of the length, but it does allow pedestrians to walk across the bridge.

The Golden Gate Bridge has had by far the most pedestrian suicides (230 versus 5), but also more vehicle-transported suicides (325 versus 107). Seiden and Spence noted that the local newspapers publicize the Golden Gate Bridge suicides but not the Bay Bridge suicides. There is even a daily unofficial lottery on the day of the week of the next suicide from the Golden Gate Bridge.

The glamor of committing suicide from the Golden Gate Bridge was illustrated by the fact that half of East Bay residents who jumped to their death crossed over the Bay Bridge to get to the Golden Gate Bridge to jump. No out-of-staters jumped from the Bay Bridge; all jumped from the Golden Gate Bridge.

What are the most "lethal" bridges in the world? I have summarized the data from the studies cited in this chapter Table 4.1. It is clear that the Golden Gate Bridge is by far the most popular bridge in the world for committing suicide and, the data appear to suggest that the bridge has become more popular over time. The number jumping each year in the 1970s is higher than the jumping over the whole life of the bridge.[1]

Table 4.1. Suicides from Bridges

Bridge	Place	Years	Suicides per Year	References
Golden Gate Bridge	San Francisco, USA	1976-1977	23.5	Kirch & Lester (1986)
		1937-1979	15.6	Seiden & Spence (1982)
		1937-1963	10.2	Lafave et al. (1995)
		1968-1981	29.6	Lafave et al. (1995)
		1982-1991	19.8	Lafave et al. (1995)
		1937-1991	19.5	Lafave et al. (1995)
Jacques Cartier Bridge	Montreal, Canada	1988-1993	9	Prevost et al. (1996)
Gateway Bridge	Brisbane, Australia	1986-1987	7.1	Cantor & Hill (1990)
Bosphorus Bridge	Istanbul, Turkey	1986-1995	6.5	Çetin et al (2001)
Clifton Suspension Bridge	Bristol, UK	1974-1993	6.4	Nowers & Gunnell (1996)
Story Bridge	Brisbane, Australia	1980-1985	3.7	Cantor & Hill (1990)
Arroyo Seco Bridge	Los Angeles, USA	1913-1936	3.5	Seiden & Spence (1982)
Aurora Bridge	Seattle, USA	1932-1981	3.1	Fortner et al. (1983)
Bay Bridge	San Francisco, USA	1937-1979	2.9	Seiden & Spence (1982)
Delaware Memorial Bridge	New Jersey/ Delaware, USA	1952-2002	2.6	Lester (2003a)
Sunshine Skyway Bridge	St Petersburg, USA	1954-2003	2.6	Lester (2005)
Sydney Harbor Bridge	Sydney, Australia	1930-1982	1.5	Harvey & Solomons (1983)

WHO JUMPS?

Which kinds of people use jumping for suicide?

There are many such studies, but let us look at just a few representative studies. Wyatt and co-workers (2000) studied suicide jumpers in southeast Scotland from 1992-1998. Of the 63 suicides, 79% were men, and 70% were judged to have a psychiatric illness. The two most frequent sites were two bridges which together accounted for 37% of the suicides, but the suicides also used high-rise car parks, homes and other buildings, and cliffs.

A similar pattern has been observed in Sweden. Lindqvist et al. (2004) studied 50 individuals who jumped off two bridges and found that they were

---

[1] An interesting illustration of the "glamor" of jumping is provided by Nicoletti (2004, 2007) on the portrayal of women jumping from bridge in London in the 1800s, when "Victorian Londoners

predominately men (64%), with a median age of 35. At least 80% had psychiatric problems, 64% had received psychiatric treatment, and 34% were in treatment at the time of their suicide. Although 27 bridges were used by these suicides, three bridges accounted for 42% of the suicides. The predominance of males was also found in suicides from the Jacques Cartier Bridge in Montreal, Canada, where 85% of the suicides were male, with an average age of 30 (Prevost et al., 1996).

In Brisbane, Australia, Cantor et al. (1989) studied suicides from the bridges for the period 1972-1987, documenting 46 suicides, 16 failed suicides, 24 attempted suicides, and 3 pranks. The suicides were primarily male, median age 31 years, never married, pensioners who were invalids, and schizophrenics. The attempted suicides were more often married, more often unemployed, less often schizophrenic and more often diagnosed with a personality disorder, and more often intoxicated. Coman et al. (2000) found that the modal jumper from the Westgate Bridge in Melbourne, Australia, in 1991–1998 was male (74%) and psychiatrically disturbed (67%), with an average age of 34.

Çetin et al. (2001) described 64 suicides from the Bosphorus Bridge in Istanbul, Turkey, in 1986–1995. Of the 65 suicides, only two survived. The typical suicide was male, 15–24 years old (younger than typical Turkish suicides), unmarried and arrived at the jumping site by taxi. The peak times were Fall and Winter and between midnight and 6 am.

The cliffs at Beach Head in England are a popular suicide venue. Surtees (1982) found that the number of suicides increased from about four per year in 1965-1969 to 13 per year in 1975-1979. The peak was on Fridays and in July and August. Males slightly outnumbered females (52% versus 48%), and the modal suicide was 25–34 years of age, from outside East Sussex (where the cliffs are located) and with a psychiatric illness (74%).

In Dade County, Florida, Copeland (1989) studied 82 suicides by jumping in 1982-1986. The majority were male (66%), white (95%), not under the influence of alcohol (76%), jumped from their homes in high-rises (65%), and depressed (62%). About a quarter (24%) had other pre-existing psychiatric conditions.

It is hard to pick out trends here. Some of the trends, such as the predominance of men and the high incidence of psychiatric disorder, are characteristic of suicides in general, by any method, and so we learn very little about jumpers from these studies. The better research compare jumpers with those using other methods for suicide.

---

were inundated with images of drowned women" such that Waterloo Bridge became known as the "Bridge of Sighs."

Jumpers versus Other Suicides

It is common to suspect that jumping from bridges and high buildings (or under trains) is a method of suicide preferred by psychiatric patients because they do not have as easy access to other methods for suicide (such as cars and guns). However, Nowers and Gunnell (1996) compared jumpers from the Clifton Suspension Bridge in Bristol, England, with suicides who used other methods. The two groups did not differ in their psychiatric history, nor in how far they lived from the bridge. However, the bridge did contribute to the local pattern of suicide since local residents were twice as likely to commit suicide by jumping as compared to elsewhere in England, and the bridge did attract those from other regions of England (about a third of the jumpers come from other regions). So in this study in England, jumpers were not more psychotic than those using other methods for suicide.

De Moore and Robertson (1999) compared *attempted suicides* by firearms and by jumping in Sydney, Australia. The jumpers were more often single, unemployed, psychotic, current inpatients or outpatients, with a past psychiatric history, who had received electro-convulsive therapy, but had no recent stressors. Those attempting suicide by firearms were more often males, substance abusers, with a criminal history, and diagnosed with borderline or antisocial personality disorder. In a multiple regression, psychosis, a psychiatric history and substance abuse predicted jumping. This study, then, leads to the opposite conclusion of that by Nowers and Gunnell reviewed above.

In Athens from 1979–1981, Kontaxakis et al. (1988) compared attempted suicides who jumped with those who took overdoses. The jumpers were more often male, married or widowed, diagnosed with schizophrenia or affective disorders (and less often with neuroses), and with somatic illnesses. The two groups did not differ in prior attempts at suicide or previous psychiatric hospitalizations. This study supports that by De Moore and Robertson.

The results of these studies are inconsistent. The two studies on attempted suicides did report an excess of psychiatrically disturbed individuals among the jumpers, but the study of completed suicides did not find such a difference. Clearly, more research on this issue is needed.

JUMPING FROM BRIDGES

Many bridges are venues for suicides, but not all receive coverage in the press. For example, Lester (2003a) documented 132 suicides during the period 1953–2002 from the Delaware Memorial Bridge which connects New Jersey and Delaware in the United States. The majority of these suicides were men (72%) and from Delaware (78%)[1], and their average age was 38. Monday was the peak day and Saturday had the fewest suicides. The suicides peaked in July and August. Suicides from this bridge receive no publicity.

There are two interesting issues about suicides by jumping from bridges.

(1) Do the suicides cluster over time, which would suggest contagion, that is, does a report on one suicide from a bridge in the news encourage others to commit suicide from the same bridge shortly after the reported suicide.

(2) What is the impact of the opening of a new bridge in a city on suicides from already existing bridges? Do potential suicides switch bridges? Does the new bridge create additional suicides?

Contagion

Since media coverage of suicide by jumping from bridges does appear to have created suicide venues, it is interesting to explore whether such suicides cluster over time. Kirch and Lester (1986) studied 47 suicides from the Golden Gate Bridge from 1976–1977, and found that the suicides were randomly distributed over the two-year period, providing no evidence for clustering.

Incidentally, Goldney (1986) noted a "spate" of suicides by jumping at a hospital in Australia in which 11 patients committed suicide by jumping in a four year period. The majority jumped from a nearby car-park garage. Kirch and Lester (1990) found no evidence of clustering in these suicides either. The suicides were randomly distributed over the four-year period.

Thus, short-term contagion appears to play no role in suicides by jumping.

---

[1] Of the two counties bordering the bridge, the Delaware county had 87% of the population.

The Availability of Bridges

Reisch et al. (2007) compared cantons in Switzerland with a high percentage of suicides jumping from bridges (mean 51.1%) with those cantons with a low percentage (mean 2.9%). Those cantons with the high percentage had a higher suicide rate by jumping (from any object), but the total suicide rate did not differ. For women, the two groups of cantons did not differ in the suicide rate by any other method. For men, however, the cantons with many bridge suicides had lower rates of suicide by overdose, suggesting switching.

Opening a New Bridge

Cantor and Hill (1990) studied the effect of the opening of a new bridge over the Brisbane River in Australia, the Gateway, in 1986. Would the suicides from the new bridge resemble those from the Story Bridge, opened in 1935? Once the two bridges were both in operation, the two groups of suicides were similar in sex, age, religion, psychiatric diagnosis, physical illness, use of alcohol and years of psychiatric contact. However, the suicides from the new bridge were less often single and unemployed. The two groups of suicides differed in where they lived— the Gateway suicides were scattered throughout the city while the Story Bridge suicides were clustered in the city core. The Gateway suicides also had fewer psychiatric admissions and fewer inpatient days. Cantor and Hill argued that, since the two groups of suicides differed, fencing in one bridge would not necessarily cause the would-be suicides from that bridge to go to the other bridge in order to jump.

The Impact of Fencing in Bridges

Two popular bridges in Washington DC in America for suicides are the Taft Bridge and the Duke Ellington Bridge over Rock Creek Park. Barriers were installed on the Duke Ellington Bridge in 1986. From 1979–1985, there were 24 suicides from the Duke Ellington Bridge, 12 from the Taft Bridge and 8 from all other bridges in the area. After barriers were installed on the Duke Ellington Bridge, from 1987–1989, there were no suicides from the Duke Ellington Bridge, 7 from the Taft Bridge and 8 from all other bridges (see Table 4.2). The average number of bridge suicides dropped from 6.3 suicides per year before the barriers were installed to 5.0 afterwards (Lester, 1993). These results are encouraging, but too small for adequate statistical tests of the change. The numbers are also too small to see whether the barrier had an impact on suicides in the city from bridges as a whole, by jumping from any place or on the overall suicide rate (O'Carroll et al., 1994).

Berman, O'Carroll and Silverman (1994) examined suicides from these same bridges. Before the barrier was erected (1979–1986), 25 suicides jumped from the Ellington Bridge and 12 from the Taft Bridge. Afterwards (1986–1990), the numbers were 1 and 10, respectively. Clearly, the barriers prevented suicides from jumping from the Ellington Bridge. However, Berman et al. pointed out that using the Taft Bridge for comparison is not methodologically sound since other possibilities (using all kinds of methods in addition to jumping) for killing yourself existed for Washington, DC residents. They noted, therefore, that an adequate study had not been done to explore whether any suicides were prevented by fencing in the Ellington Bridge or whether potential suicides simply switched methods.

Table 4.2. The results of fencing in the Duke Ellington Bridge in Washington, DC

		Ellington Bridge (per year)	Taft Bridge (per year)	Other Bridges (per year)	Total (per year)
Lester (1993)					
1979–1985	7 years	3.4	1.7	1.1	6.3
1987–1989	3 years	0	2.3	2.7	5
Berman et al. (1994)					
1979–1986	8 years	3.7	1.7	?	
1986–1990	5 years	0.2	2	?	

In England and Wales, barriers were erected on the Clifton Suspension Bridge in 1998. Bennewith et al. (2007) compared suicide in the region for the five years prior to this and for the five years afterwards. The number of bridge suicides was cut in half, from 8.2 per year to 4.0. Suicides by jumping from other sites increased from 6.2 to 8.4, a non-significant increase and a result of the increase in suicides by jumping by women in the region (and in the whole of England and

Wales). (In the five years prior to the erection of the barrier on the bridge, only one out of the 41 suicides was female.) The number of suicides per year from jumping from any site dropped from 14.4 to 12.4 (a non-significant change), while the suicide rate in the area declined from 11.2 per 100,000 per year to 10.5, a non-significant decline. Thus, erecting barriers on the bridge reduced suicides from the bridge and does not appear to have been accompanied by displacement to other methods for suicide.

Pelletier (2007) compared suicide by jumping from the Memorial Bridge in Augusta, Maine, before and after the installation of safety fences in 1983. From 1960 to 1982, there were 14 suicides from the bridge versus none afterwards (from 1984 to 2005). During these same two periods, there were 9 and 9 suicides by jumping from a high place in Augusta (other than from the Memorial Bridge), respectively, which indicates that those who might have jumped to their death from the Memorial Bridge did not jump from other high places.

Reisch and Michel (2005) investigated the impact of placing a fence on part of the Berne Muenster Terrace in 1998 in Switzerland which is in a park overlooking a river and part of the old town and which had become a "hot spot" for suicides. The fence was built to protect those under the bridge from injury and psychological trauma caused by the suicides. However, the fence did not enclose all of the possible places in the park from which to jump, and there were other bridges visible from the park which could be used for suicide. Despite this, whereas six persons jumped in the four years before the erection of the fence, none did so in the four years afterwards. Surprisingly, the number of suicides by jumping from any place in Berne declined after the erection of the fence. Reisch and Michel suggested that the fence not only prevented suicides from that place, but had a psychological impact on suicide by jumping in general. Reisch and Michel noted also that media reports in Berne about suicide by jumping increased in the years before the installation of the fence and declined thereafter. Media publicity may, therefore, have played a role in the decline of suicide by jumping. Unfortunately, Reisch and Michel did not carry out any statistical tests of whether suicides in Berne switched to other methods for suicide after the fence was installed.

Removing Barriers

Beautrais (2001) took advantage of a decision by a town council in somewhere in Australia or New Zealand (Beautrais did not want to name the town) to remove safety barriers from a bridge on the grounds that (i) they were unsightly, (ii) they impeded rescue efforts, and (iii) they did not prevent suicide. In the four-year periods before and after the removal of the barriers, the number of suicides increased from 3 to 15, with estimated rates of 0.29 per 100,000 per year before removal of the barrier, rising to 1.29 afterwards.

Beautrais also looked for switching. Did more suicides occur by jumping elsewhere in the city? Focusing on the two-year periods before and after removal of the barriers, the number of suicides by jumping remained constant (14 in each two-year period), but the location did switch to the newly unfenced bridge, a change that was statistically significant. These data suggest that switching did occur.

Beautrais noted that the majority of the suicides from the bridge were men, schizophrenics and either inpatients or in residential care at the time. Those jumping from other sites included more women, were somewhat older and were somewhat less likely to be schizophrenics or psychiatric inpatients, but the numbers were too small for reliable conclusions to be drawn about the differences in the two groups. If the groups did differ in characteristics, then this would argue against switching. Instead, the removal of the safety barriers may have increased the rate of suicide among some groups of the population (in this case, schizophrenics).

Call Boxes and a Police Presence

Glatt (1987; Glatt et al., 1986) studied the effect of putting two suicide prevention telephones on the Mid-Hudson Bridge in Poughkeepsie, New York. In the first two years, the telephones were used 30 times, and only one of these callers jumped. Nine other people did not use the telephones, and five of these jumped. Thus, it is clear that the telephones were used, but unfortunately Glatt did not present any data on the number of jumpers prior to and after the telephone were installed.

The Sunshine Skyway Bridge in St. Petersburg, Florida, provides a 155-foot plunge (Lester, 2005). The bridge opened in 1954 and the first suicides occurred in November 1957. Since then, 127 suicides have occurred from the bridge. In the year 2000, the Florida state police began staffing the bridge full-time, and one officer reported talking seven suicides out of jumping while 19 others did jump.

Six emergency call boxes were placed on the bridge after July 1999, which connect directly to the Crisis Center in Tampa and also alert the bridge police. Since then, 18 people have called, and none of these jumped. From 1996–1998,

25 suicides took placed from the bridge; from 2000-2002, 19 suicides took place. These numbers are too small to detect a significant change.

Switching

To try to see if jumpers will switch methods for suicide, Seiden (1978) compared a group of jumpers from the Golden Gate Bridge who were restrained with a group of attempted suicides seen at a local hospital. During the follow-up period, 12.5% of the 515 Golden Gate individuals died (with a median follow-up period of 27 years) as compared to 25.5% of the 184 attempted suicides (with a median follow-up period of 15 years). Twenty-five of the 64 deaths from the bridge individuals were from suicide (with seven jumping from the bridge) as compared to 13 of the 47 attempted suicides. Given the longer follow-up of the bridge individuals, their suicide rate was less than that of the attempted suicides. Seiden concluded that the vast majority (95%) of bridge individuals did not commit suicide. While of interest, these results are not good evidence for switching versus not-switching to other methods for suicide.

Rosen (1975) interviewed six jumpers who survived a jump from the Golden Gate Bridge. All six said that their suicide plan involved only the Golden Gate Bridge, and four said that they would not have switched bridges if the Golden Gate Bridge had been fenced in. In a two and a half year follow-up, only one of the six made a second suicide attempt. All favored fencing in the Golden Gate Bridge and advocated less newspaper coverage of jumpers from the bridge.

Interestingly, Miller et al. (2006) surveyed Americans and found that 34% believed that, if a suicide barrier was placed on the Golden Gate Bridge, every potential suicide would kill themselves by another method, and an additional 40% believed that most of the potential suicides would have killed themselves using another method. Thus, the general public thinks that switching is likely.

JUMPING FROM BUILDINGS

Salmons (1984) studied psychiatric patients who jumped to their death from a psychiatric ward at a Birmingham, England, hospital from 1963-1981, after which, on the recommendation of the coroner, the ward was closed. Fourteen of the 17 suicides were psychiatric patients while three were medical or surgical patients. Seven were men and six women, and the modal age was 16–25. None occurred from 6 pm to midnight. Salmons' study points to the inappropriateness of allowing psychiatric patients access to a high place from which to jump in the hospital. Amazingly, the hospital did not close that ward until the coroner pointed this out.

Yip and Tan (1998) compared suicide in Singapore and Hong Kong, both densely populated countries with many high-rise buildings. From 1984 to 1994, the rates of suicide who used jumping increased, from 4.1 per 1000,000 per year to 7.2 in Hong Kong, and from 5.7 to 7.1 in Singapore. In contrast, suicides in Taiwan hardly ever used jumping for suicide - 3 percent in 1999 as compared to 59 percent in Hong Kong in the same year (Yip et al., 1996).

However, there were differences in the two countries. The *suicide rate* from jumping in Hong Kong increased steadily over the ten-year period, while the suicide rate by jumping in Singapore peaked in 1989 and declined thereafter. Whereas the *proportion* of suicides by jumping increased steadily over the ten-year period in Hong Kong, the proportion remained steady in Singapore.

Lester (1994) found a positive association between the percentage of people living in high-rise buildings in Singapore from 1960 to 1976 and suicides by jumping from high-rises (see Table 4.3). The suicide rate by jumping rose so much that, despite a drop in suicide rates by all other methods, the total suicide rate rose during this period. This suggests that the building of high-rises created new suicides in addition to leading potential suicides to switch methods.

Table 4.3. Suicide in Singapore

	1960	**1976**
Percent of the population living in high-rises	9.10%	51.00%
Total suicide rate	8.6	11.2
Suicide rate by jumping	1.4	5.7
Suicide rate by other methods	7.2	5.5
Percent of suicides by jumping	17%	51%

Do those who are psychiatric disturbed use jumping more for suicide in these countries? Kua and Tsoi (1985) found a tendency for suicides with a psychiatric history to use jumping more in Singapore in 1980 (68% versus 57%), but the difference was not statistically significant.

Marzuk et al. (1992) compared suicide rates by each method in the five counties of New York City in 1984–1987. For methods with equal access across the counties, such as hanging and cutting/piercing, there were no differences in suicide rates. The two counties with the most high-rise buildings (Manhattan and the Bronx) had much higher suicide rates by jumping than the other three counties. (The five counties also differed in suicide rates by car exhaust, prescribed medications, trains and subways, methods for which the availability also differed by county.)

A similar study was carried out by Fischer et al. (1993). They examined suicides in New York City in 1984–1985. Most of those using jumping for suicide jumped from their own residence (81%) and from a window (58%). Those living in buildings with 13 or more floors were 11 times more likely to use jumping for suicide, while those with access to medication were half as likely to use jumping. Suicides in psychiatric hospitals were seven times more likely to use jumping, while those who were substance abusers were one-third as likely to use jumping. Jumping was more likely as a method for suicide for those living in the borough of Manhattan and the Bronx (where there were more high buildings). Jumping was also more common for men, the never married and those living alone.

OTHER ISSUES

There are two other issues of interest that can be looked at using suicide by jumping: are there sex differences in the outcome and the reactions of bystanders.

There is strong sex difference in suicidal behavior in which men are more likely to make lethal suicidal acts and die (completed suicide) while women are more likely to make non-lethal suicidal acts and survive (attempted suicide). One explanation for this sex difference is that women choose less lethal methods for suicide (Lester, 1984). However, Lester showed that, within each method of suicide, men are more likely to die while women are more likely to survive.

Lester (1990) examined data from Katz and co-workers (1988) who reported on the injuries sustained by attempted suicides who jumped from 6 to 12 meters. The men and women jumped from similar heights and sustained similarly severe injuries. Thus, there was no evidence that women jump from lower heights or are physiologically more able to resist injury. Lester (2003b) found that men and women in India jumping to their death jump from similar heights. Lester (2007) reviewed several previous studies and found no differences in any of them in the heights from which men and women jump. However, the survival rate was better from women jumping from the Aurora Bridge in Seattle than for men. The women were younger than the men, and so age must be controlled for in future research.

What is the reaction bystanders to jumpers? Mann (1981) documented 10 cases (out of 21 situations) where the crowds who gathered when a person was threatening to jump off a building or bridge baited or jeered the jumper. This was more common at night, in the summer months, and if the situation had a long duration.

A CASE STUDY

In June 1997, the Schizophrenia Society of Ontario endeavored to get the Bloor Street Viaduct in Toronto fenced in, to prevent people jumping to their death from it, after they had learned that four of their members had committed suicide from the bridge.[1,2] This bridge, formerly known as the Prince Edward Viaduct, had been the site for 74 suicides and 16 attempts since 1990.[3] On October 30, 1997, Martin Kruze, a 35-year-old man who went public with his experiences as a teenager of sexual abuse at the hands of employees at the Toronto Maple Leaf Gardens, committed suicide from the bridge. Several suicides followed in the next few weeks, including a 17-year-old student at St. Michael's Choir School.[4]

Other strategies proposed for suicide prevention at the Bloor Street Viaduct included emergency telephones distributed across the bridge, police and community patrols, and changing the public perception of the bridge. There are reports of other bridges with telephones: the Mid-Hudson Bridge in Poughkeepsie (NY), the Coronado Bridge in San Diego (CA), the Golden Gate Bridge in San Francisco (CA), the Howard Taft Bridge (DC), the Gateway Bridge in Brisbane (Australia), the Clifton Suspension Bridge, Bristol (UK) and the Erskine Bridge (Scotland). There is also a bridge patrol for the Golden Gate Bridge.

Different groups lined up on the two sides. In opposition were the Toronto Historical Board and right-to-die groups. In favor were the Toronto Police Department and mental health groups. The Schizophrenia Society solicited letters

---

[1] There is also danger from the suicides to cars passing under the bridge.

[2] The Psychiatric Foundation of Northern California also played a role in efforts to get the Golden Gate Bridge fenced in (Hutchings et al., 2007).

[3] The figures 37 and 93 have also appeared in newspaper reports. About 300 people have jumped since its construction in 1919. It accounts for half of all bridge suicides in Toronto.

[4] New York State requires bridges and overpasses to have safety fences, and a mesh screen was erected on both sides of the Glen Street Bridge (Glen Falls, NY) after a young male epileptic jumped from it (and maimed himself). As we have noted above, the Duke Ellington Bridge in Washington, DC was fitted with fences in 1986.

of support from experts, including Dr. Isaac Sakinofsky at the local Clarke Institute of Psychiatry and myself.

Opponents argued that people would simply switch methods if the bridge was fenced in, fencing would deface this landmark bridge, the money involved could be put to better use, and the measure would lead to all bridges being fenced in.

A petition obtained 1,200 signatures, and supporters visited over 46 city councillors in the winter of 1998 to solicit their support. On July 8, 1998, the 57-member city council voted unanimously to hold a design competition for the fence. $1.5 million was budgeted for the fences and telephones. A luminous veil design from Derek Revington won, and the council approved the design on October 1, 1998.

A subway track runs under the road level of the bridge, and the Toronto Transit Commission objected to the barrier since it would interfere with their inspection of the track which was done by means of a truck parked on the road level with an articulated arm.

The Schizophrenia Society and its supporters worked hard to gather support for the fencing. On March 31, 1999, the Urban Environment and Development Committee approved funds for a modified truck for the Transit Commission. The architects increased their estimates of the cost of the fencing to $2.2 million, and on May 12, 1999, the Council approved this. Construction of the fence was to have been completed by 2000.

But, then, in the fall of 1999, the bids for the bridge came in at $5.5 million, and the new Works Committee was composed of city councillors unfamiliar with the project. The Schizophrenia Society once more had to seek support for the project, both in the local community and from experts around the world. The project was once more on-hold.

The safety fence (called The Luminous Veil) was finally funded in 2001 and completed in 2003, after six years of effort by proponents of the fence. As of 2005, there had been no suicides since its construction. As of 2008, the effort to have fences or barriers installed on the Golden Gate Bridge continue. Two facts are important here. First, the Luminous Veil received a Canadian national engineering award for design excellence and is thought to have improved the aesthetics of the Bloor street viaduct. Second, with regard to cost, John Bateson of the Contra Costa Crisis Center has pointed out that cost was not an issue when $5 million was spent to build a barrier to separate cyclists from cars on the Golden Gate Bridge (no cyclists have ever been killed on the bridge), nor when a meridian was installed to prevent head-on collisions (from which there had been only 40 fatalities as compared to 1,300 suicides).

Hutchings et al. (2007) have played a role in efforts to get fences installed for the Golden Gate Bridge and presented an approach (a decision matrix) for similar efforts. They examined the trade-off between cost and effectiveness and between cost and aesthetic interests, and they also took into account aerodynamic performance and structural performance of the barriers. Their discussion will prove useful in future efforts to have fences installed at other suicide venues.

DISCUSSION

Gunnell and Nowers (1997) reviewed the published studies on suicide by jumping. They noted that the proportion of men to women jumping varied greatly, with men predominating in America, for example, and women in Switzerland.

Less consistently, the psychiatrically disturbed do seem to use jumping from bridges and other structures (other than from the buildings in their psychiatric institutions) more than other suicides, but Gunnell and Nowers note that some bridges and buildings may be closer to psychiatric facilities than others, and this may account for the inconsistency in the results. The incidence of schizophrenia in the samples of the jumpers in the research reviewed ranged from 10% to 45% and of depression from 13% to 67%. Follow-up studies of jumpers who survive give varying estimates of the likelihood of subsequent attempted and completed suicide.

We can draw several conclusions from the research reviewed in this chapter. First, among attempted suicides, those who are psychiatric patients (past or present) do seem to prefer jumping as a method for suicide. Whether this is true for completed suicides is unclear at the present time. It is thought that potential suicides who are psychiatrically disturbed choose jumping because they do not have easy access to guns and medications to kill themselves, but there has never been research to test this explanation.

Second, fencing in bridges does prevent suicides from those bridges. The evidence for switching is not clear at the present time, primarily because the use of jumping for suicide is a relatively rare choice of method. The data from Singapore, however, does suggest that the growth in the number of high rise buildings did create additional suicides.

A FINAL COMMENT

We noted above that in the 1990s, the Schizophrenia Society of Ontario pressed for a safety fence for the Bloor Street Viaduct in Toronto, Canada. The city council kept putting a decision off. Various excuses were given: it was too expensive, it would mar the beauty of the bridge, etc. A large proportion of those who jump from bridges and buildings are psychiatric patients, and it is noteworthy that it was a self-help group of schizophrenics who agitated for this bridge to be made safe.

It is also noteworthy that, in a world where governments in many countries act in a paternalistic way to restrict individual freedoms in the name of safety (laws require motor cyclists to wear helmets, car drivers to buckle-up their seat belts, and children in cars to be placed in safety seats), local governments delay and sometimes prevent safety measures for bridges. Certainly, any psychiatric hospital (or, indeed, other building) that failed to enclose stairwells and restrict access to the roof would be held liable for patient suicides. Indeed, any building that experienced a suicide (for example from its roof or inside an atrium) and failed to modify the building could be held legally liable.

The research reviewed in this chapter has studied occasional instances where one bridge in a city is fenced in, but all the others are left unfenced. This is foolish. All the bridges should be fenced in. In the United States, the majority of roads and footpaths crossing the major interstate highways are fenced in to prevent people throwing stones or rocks at the cars passing underneath. Yet, cities will not fence in bridges to prevent suicides from jumping from them. The logic behind such different decisions is hard to fathom.

If you have a swimming pool in the United States and do not fence it in, and if a child drowns in your pool, you will lose the lawsuit brought by the parents of the victim. Perhaps if we held legislators personally accountable, the bridges would be quickly be fenced in.

REFERENCES

Beautrais, A. L. (2001). Effectiveness of barriers at suicide jumping sites. *Australian & New Zealand Journal of Psychiatry*, 35, 557-562.

Bennewith, O., Nowers, M., & Gunnell, D. (2007). Effect of barriers on the Clifton suspension bridge, England, on local patterns of suicide. *British Journal of Psychiatry*, 190,266-267.

Berman, A. L., O'Carroll, P. W., & Silverman, M. M. (1994). Community suicide prevention. *Suicide & Life-Threatening Behavior*, 24, 89-99.

Cantor, C. H., & Hill, M. A. (1990). Suicide from river bridges. *Australian & New Zealand Journal of Psychiatry*, 24, 377-380.

Cantor, C. H., Hill, M. A., & McLachlan, E. K. (1989). Suicide and related behaviour from river bridges. *British Journal of Psychiatry*, 155, 829-835.

Çetin, G., Gunay, Y., Fincanci, S. K., & Kolusayin, R. O. (2001). Suicides by jumping from Bosphorus Bridge in Istanbul. *Forensic Science International*, 116, 157-162.

Coman, M., Meyer, A. D. M., & Cameron, P. A. (2000). Jumping from the Westgate Bridge, Melbourne. *Medical Journal of Australia*, 172, 67-69.

Copeland, A. R. (1989). Suicide by jumping from buildings. *American Journal of Forensic Medicine & Pathology*, 1989, 10, 295-298.

De Moore, G. M., & Robertson, A. R. (1999). Suicide attempts by firearms and by leaping from heights. *American Journal of Psychiatry*, 156, 1425-1431.

Derobert, L., Hadengue, A., Proteau, J., & Schaub, S. (1965). Doit-on supprimer la Tour Eiffel? *Annales de Medecine Legale, Criminologie, Police Scientifique, et Toxicologie*, 45, 115-119.

Ellis, E. R., & Allen, G. N. (1961). *Traitor within*. Garden City, NY: Doubleday.

Fischer, E. P., Comstock, G. W., Monk, M. A., & Sencer, D. J. (1993). Characteristics of completed suicides. *Suicide & Life-Threatening Behavior*, 23, 91-100.

Fortner, G. S., Oreskovich, M. R., Copass, M. K., & Carrico, C. J. (1983). The effects of prehospital trauma on survival from a 50-meter fall. *Journal of Trauma*, 23, 976-981.

Glatt, K. M. (1987). Helpline. *Suicide & Life-Threatening Behavior* 17, 299-309.

Glatt, K. M., Sherwood, D. W., & Amisson, T. J. (1986). Telephone helplines at a suicide site. *Hospital & Community Psychiatry*, 37, 178-180.

Goldney, R. D. (1986). A spate of suicide by jumping. *Australian Journal of Social Issues*, 21, 119-125.

Gunnell, D., & Nowers, M. (1997). Suicide by jumping. *Acta Psychiatrica Scandinavica*, 96, 1-6.

Hanzlick, R., Masterson, K., & Waker, B. (1990). Suicide by jumping from high-rise hotels. *American Journal of Forensic Medicine & Pathology*, 1990, 11, 294-297.

Harvey, P. M., & Solomons, B. J. (1983). Survival after free falls of 59 meters into water from the Sydney Harbour Bridge. *Medical Journal of Australia*, 1, 504-511.

Hutchings, D., Simpson, R., Stauffer, R., & Wahl, D. (2007). Aesthetics, death, and landmark structures. *Journal of Architectural Engineering*, 13, 1-8.

Katz, K., Gonen, N., Goldberg, I., Mizrahi, J., Radwan, M., & Yosipovitch, Z. (1988). Injuries in attempted suicide by jumping from a height. *Injury*, 19, 371-374.

Kirch, M. R., & Lester, D. (1986). Suicide from the Golden Gate Bridge. *Psychological Reports*, 59, 1314.

Kirch, M. R., & Lester, D. (1990). Is a spate of suicides a cluster? *Perceptual & Motor Skills*, 70, 46.

Kontaxakis, V., Markidis, M., Vaslamatzis, G., Ioannidis, H., & Stefanis, C. (1988). Attempted suicide by jumping. *Acta Psychiatrica Scandinavica*, 77, 435-437.

Kua, E. H., & Tsoi, W. F. (1985). Suicide in the island of Singapore. *Acta Psychiatrica Scandinavica*, 71, 227-229.

Lafave, M., Hutton, J., LaPorta, A. J., & Mallory, P. L. (1995). History of high-velocity impact water trauma at Letterman Army Medical Center. *Military Medicine*, 160, 197-199.

Lester, D. (1984). Suicide. In C. S. Widom (Ed.) *Sex roles and psychopathology*, pp. 145-156. New York: Plenum.

Lester, D. (1990). Sex differences in severity of injury in attempted suicides who jump. *Perceptual & Motor Skills*, 71, 176.

Lester, D. (1993). Suicide from bridges in Washington, DC. *Perceptual & Motor Skills*, 77, 534.

Lester, D. (1994). Suicide by jumping in Singapore as a function of high-rise apartment availability. *Perceptual & Motor Skills*, 79, 74.

Lester, D. (2003a). Suicide by jumping from a bridge. *Perceptual & Motor Skills*, 97, 338.

Lester, D. (2003b). Do male and female suicides jump from different heights? *Perceptual & Motors Skills*, 96, 798.

Lester, D. (2005). Suicide by jumping from bridges. *Perceptual & Motors Skills*, 100, 628.

Lester, D. (2007). Sex differences in surviving suicide attempts by jumping. *Psychological Reports*, 100, 1121-1122.

Lester, D., & Brockopp, G. W. (1971). Niagara Falls suicides. *Journal of the American Medical Association*, 1971, 215, 797-798.

Lester, D., & Jason, D. (1989). Suicides at the casino. *Psychological Reports*, 64, 337-338.

Lindqvist, P., Jonsson, A., Eriksson, A., Hedelin, A., & Bjornstig, U. (2004). Are suicides by jumping off bridges preventable? *Accident Analysis & Prevention*, 36, 691-694.

Mann, L. (1981). The baiting crowd in episodes of threatened suicide. *Journal of Personality & Social Psychology*, 41, 703-709.

Marzuk, P. M., Leon, A. C., Tardiff, K., Morgan, E. B., Stajic, M., & Mann, J. J. (1992). The effect of access to lethal methods of injury on suicide rates. *Archives of General Psychiatry*, 49, 451-458.

Miller, M., Azrael, D., & Hemenway, D. (2006). Belief in the inevitability of suicide. *Suicide & Life-Threatening Behavior*, 36, 1-11.

Nicoletti, L. J. (2004). Downward mobility: Victorian women, suicide, and London's "Bridge of Sighs." *Literary London*, 2(1), retrieved online from www.literarylondon/london-journal/march2004/nicoletti.html.

Nicoletti, L. J. (2007). Morbid topographies: Placing suicide in Victorian London. In L. Phillips (Ed.) *A mighty mass of brick and mortar*, pp. 7-34. (*DQR Studies in Literature 41*). Amsterdam/New York: Rodopi.

Nowers, M., & Gunnell, D. (1996). Suicide from the Clifton Suspension Bridge in England. *Journal of Epidemiology & Community Health*, 50, 30-32.

O'Carroll, P. W., Silverman, M. M., & Berman, A. L. (1994). Community suicide prevention. *Suicide & Life-Threatening Behavior*, 24, 89-99.

Pelletier, A. R. (2007). Preventing suicide by jumping. *Injury Prevention*, 13, 57-59.

Prevost, C., Julien, M., & Brown, B. P. (1996). Suicides associated with the Jacques Cartier Bridge, Montreal, Quebec 1988-1993. *Canadian Journal of Public Health*, 87, 377-380.

Reisch, T., & Michel, K. (2005). Securing a suicide hot spot. *Suicide & Life-Threatening Behavior*, 35, 460-467.

Reisch, T., Schuster, U., & Michel, K. (2007). Suicide by jumping and accessibility of bridges. *Suicide & Life-Threatening Behavior*, 37, 681-687.

Rosen, D. (1975). Suicide survivors. *Western Journal of Medicine*, 122, 289-294.

Ross, T. E., & Lester, D. (1991). Suicides at Niagara Falls. *American Journal of Public Health*, 81, 1677-1678.

Salmons, P. H. (1984). Suicide in high buildings. *British Journal of Psychiatry*, 145, 469-472.

Seiden, R. H. (1978). Where are they now? *Suicide & Life-Threatening Behavior*, 8, 203-216.

Seiden, R. H., & Spence, M. (1982). A tale of two bridges. *Crisis*, 3(1), 32-40.

Seiden, R. H., & Spence, M. (1983-1984). A tale of two bridges. *Omega*, 14, 201-209.

Simpson, M. A. (1978). The great suicide epidemic of 1933. *World Medicine*, September 6, 77-79.

Surtees, S. J. (1982). Suicide and accidental death at Beachy Head. *British Medical Journal*, 284, 321-324.

Wyatt, J. P., Beale, J. P., Graham, C. A., Beard, D., & Busuttil, A. (2000). Suicidal high falls. *Journal of Clinical Forensic Medicine*, 7, 1-5.

Yip, P. S. F. (1996). Suicides in Hong Kong, Taiwan and Beijing. *British Journal of Psychiatry*, 169, 495-500.

Yip, P. S. F., & Tan, R. C. E. (1998). Suicides in Hong-Kong and Singapore. *International Journal of Social Psychiatry*, 44, 267-279.

Chapter 5

TRAINS

The reason I did it at [the busiest] station is that I wanted the most number of
people to know that I killed myself...when I jumped I felt full of hate for
everyone in the world...I wanted to punish the whole world...I wanted everyone
to know how unhappy I was, how much I had suffered.

— Guggenheim & Weisman, 1972, p. 408

Suicide by jumping in front of a train or subway car has not been a popular
method of suicide, but it is quite lethal (more than 90% die). Those who survive
often sustain severe damage, sometimes requiring amputation of mangled limbs.
Trains suicide has also resulted in "suicide venues." For example, the numbers of
suicides on JR East's railway network in Japan increased from 81 a year in 1990
to 212 in 1999. A railway crossing in Kunitachi City became a popular site. The
company began painting the railroad crossing gates bright green to try to change
the potential suicide's mood, and to install mirrors across the tracks from
platforms so that jumpers could see themselves which might make them pause
(French, 2000).

RAILWAYS

In Germany, Schmidtke (1994) studied 6,090 suicides on the railroads from
1976-1984. The modal railway suicide was male, aged 20-29 for men and 40-49
for women, taking place in the station. The number declined in December, on

weekends, and from midnight to 6 a.m. Only 391 (6.0%) people made suicide attempts (and survived) on the railroads during this time period, indicating that this is a lethal method for suicide from which few survive (especially if made outside of the station).

Radbo et al. (2005) studied 145 railway suicides in Sweden from 2000-2002. The modal suicide was male, 20-59 years of age, and occurred more during the warmer months, less often on weekends and less often at night. The majority of the suicides were standing, walking, lying or sitting on the tracks, typically outside of the station area. Radbo et al. suggested that systems to detect people on the tracks would give drivers more time to apply their brakes. Since 54% of the suicides occurred in the three urban areas (Stockholm, Gothenburg and Malmo), such a system could be deployed most efficiently in these three urban areas.

In the southern region of England, Symonds (1985, 1994) found 80 probable suicides in a two year period on the railroads, and the number seemed to have increased during the 1970s. These suicides were predominantly men, but younger than other suicides. About two-thirds had given a clear indication of suicidal intent, 43% had an affective disorder and 15% had schizophrenia or paranoid states. As compared to the accidental deaths, the suicides were younger, the men less often married and the women more often married, and both sexes less often widowed. The suicides were more often psychiatrically disturbed but less often alcoholics. The incidence of suicide did not seem to be related to the volume of passengers, residence in a rail-dense area, location in areas with high suicide rates or the proximity of a psychiatric hospital.

De Leo and Krysinska (2008) identified 8,220 suicides in Queensland, Australia, from 1990-2004, of whom 161 used trains - a suicide rate by this method of 0.32 per 100,000 per year. They also identified 18 attempted suicides. The modal train suicide was male, aged 15-34, unmarried and not employed. About a third were known to have consumed alcohol prior to their suicide, and 40% had a psychiatric disorder, most commonly unipolar depression and psychosis. About one fifth were known to have previously attempted suicide. Ten of the suicides completed suicide while AWOL from a psychiatric ward. Seventy-three percent occurred on the rails away from stations, 47% by lying or sitting on the tracks, 21% jumped or ran in front of the train, and 20% occurred while the individual was walking or standing on the tracks. Only two suicides drove their car into a train. Several "hot spots" were identified – 13 stations accounted for a third of all suicides. In an earlier study, Emmerson and Cantor (1993) found that 57% of railway suicides in Brisbane in Queensland were diagnosed as schizophrenics and 57% were inpatients at the time of their suicide.

Van Houwelingen and Kerkhof (2008) studied the psychiatric status of 57 suicides by train in the Netherlands and reviewed four other studies (from Australia, Denmark and the UK). The proportion with a psychiatric history ranged from 60% to 83%; combining all the data (for 262 train suicides) gave a proportion of 65%, not very different from suicides in the general population by other methods. Overall, 53% were receiving psychiatric care of some kind at the time of the suicide and 49% of those receiving psychiatric were in-patients, and these percentages were much higher than suicides in the general population by other methods. Overall, only 13% had no psychiatric diagnosis, 39% had an affective disorder, 25% a psychosis, and 23% an "other" diagnosis.

Clarke (1994) studied railway suicides in England and Wales and found that the number of people completing suicide using trains over time from 1820 to1949 was positively associated with the length of railway track and number of passengers carried on the system.

In Germany from 1991 to 2000, Baumert et al. (2005) noted that the absolute length of railway track declined while the distance travelled by trains and the distance travelled by passengers increased. The number of railway suicides increased during this period, both absolutely and as a proportion of all suicides. While the general suicide rate declined during the period, the railway suicide rate stayed constant.

There are many other epidemiological studies of suicides on the railroads (for a review see Krysinsak & De Leo [2008]), but there are no simple tactics available for preventing these suicides, nor has there been any empirical test of their effectiveness. Kerkhof (2003) suggested the following measures:

1. Installing fences along railroad tracks to prevent access
2. Better maintenance of existing fences
3. Use of (visible) cameras at railroad crossings and on platforms combined with signals and megaphones
4. Installation of alarm buttons on stations so that the public can raise the alarm if they see someone behaving dangerously
5. Modification of the front of trains to minimize damage to people

A further measure might be:

6. The installation of sensors on trains to detect and warn drivers of a person on the track so that they can begin braking. Analogous technology is

installed on some cars so that drivers can detect animals on the road in time to brake.

Suicides in subway transit systems are more amenable to prevention. Let us consider these suicides.

SUBWAY SYSTEMS

Epidemiology

Guggenheim and Weisman (1972) examined 50 incidents in the Boston subway and distinguished jumpers (32 cases), prostraters (who lay on the tracks) (6 cases), touchers (5 cases) and wanderers (7 cases). Only 34% died, but almost all the fatalities were from the jumpers (94%). Fifty two percent of the cases were males, 50% living apart from their family, 62% not currently married, and 59% unemployed or retired.

Fifty six percent had been psychiatrically hospitalized in the past, 16% currently, and 8% pending; 28% were diagnosed as having an affective disorder and 14% schizophrenia; 40% were acute or chronic alcoholics. Thirty-three survivors were followed up for an average of 5½ years, and only one completed suicide, though some others did make suicide attempts.

Guggenheim and Weisman noted that many of the persons were trying to avoid help - by *not* communicating their suicidal intent to significant others, by fighting with rescuers, and occasionally having the suicidal action triggered by an offer of hospitalization of psychiatric help. Many of the people were also aware of the public nature of their action and desired this (see the quote at the beginning of the chapter).

Johnston and Waddell (1984) studied suicidal behavior in the Toronto subway system which opened in 1954. From 1954-1980, there were 207 completed suicides and 223 attempted suicides. The rate of completed suicide increased during the 1970s, peaked in November and December and around midday, and in those in their 20s. Suicides occurred more often in the older stations (of course, since they had been open for a longer period), in transfer stations and in those near psychiatric facilities. Seventy-three (61%) of a sample of 119 suicides had a psychiatric history, most often depression, followed by schizophrenia. Of these 73 cases, 40% had made prior attempts, 10% had eloped from a psychiatric ward, and 26% were psychiatric outpatients.

Johnston and Waddell suggested double-door (or sliding curtain) subway stations as a means of preventing these suicides. They also noted a subway train weighs 180 tons and travels at 45 miles per hour when entering the station. It takes 400 feet to stop such a train. They suggested that slowing train speeds when entering the station to 10 miles per hour would make fatal injuries less probable.

Farmer et al. (1991) gathered data for the London Tube system for 1940-1989. The number of "incidents" increased during this period, while the proportion of these incidents that were fatal declined. The percentage of fatalities that were judged to be suicides remained roughly constant over the period, after taking into account the tendency of English coroners to disguise suicides by classifying them as "undetermined."

On the whole, the stations with more passenger throughput had more incidents, with two exceptions, both of which were close to psychiatric units. At these two stations, the proportion of victims who were inpatients was 55% and 22%.

Farmer et al. made recommendations for preventing suicide in subway stations. They noted that the survival rate for stations with a channel several feet deep under the rails was 55% compared to only 32% in stations without this "suicide pit." (Coats and Walter [1999] found a difference of 56% versus 24% for 58 incidents in the London Underground in 1996-1997.) They also noted that the Singapore subway system had doors on platforms that matched the positioning of the doors on the stopped trains, and the system has had no suicides. (This was done so as to preserve energy in the air-conditioned stations) They also suggested putting "skirts" on the trains to prevent bodies going under the wheels.

Gaylord and Lester (1994) studied suicides on the Hong Kong Subway from 1979-1991, during which there were 56 suicides and 76 suicide attempts. The modal suicide was male, with an average age of 38 for the men and 30 for the women. The peak time was 11 a.m. to 3 p.m. The number of suicides and attempts rose with increasing passenger traffic until 1986, but declined thereafter, perhaps as the staff implemented suicide prevention surveillance measures (see below).

O'Donnell and Farmer (1992) surveyed 23 subway systems. Overall, the number of incidents per year was more strongly associated with the number of stations in the system than with the passenger traffic. The modal suicide was aged 21-30 and male. Fatality rates ranged from 20% in Nuremburg (Germany) to 80% in Mexico City. The peak time was late morning and early afternoon, but there were no consistent daily or seasonal trends. The fatality rate was associated with both the number of passengers carried by the system and the number of stations, but more strongly with the latter. Fatality rates were greater in systems without suicide pits and lower if the trains had rubber tires (which facilitates braking).

(The use of rubber tires may account for the low fatality rate on the Paris Metro system [O'Donnell & Farmer, 1992].) Lester (1995) compared the subway suicide rates for 17 of the cities studied by O'Donnell and Farmer with the national suicide rates and found no association.

O'Donnell and Farmer (1994) examined suicides on the London underground system and found that stations with higher passenger flow had more suicides, as did those near to psychiatric hospitals (after controlling for passenger flow). The fatality rate was greater in stations with no suicide pit (66%) versus those with a suicide pit (45%). Those jumping from the first third of the platform were also more often fatal (68%) than those from the middle third (48%) and those from the final third (27%).

Accessibility

Marzuk et al. (1992) compared suicide rates by each method in the five counties of New York City in 1984-1987. For methods with equal access across the counties, such as hanging and cutting/piercing, there were no differences in suicide rates. Subway suicides occurred at the highest rates in Manhattan and the Bronx and at the lowest rate in Staten Island. Train suicides occurred at the highest rate in Queens and the Bronx. These differences were found to be associated with the density of people in the five counties living close to subways and train lines. For example, Manhattan has the highest density of subway stations (6.4 per square mile) as compared to 2.1 in Brooklyn and zero in Staten Island. The Bronx has 0.41% of the population living with ½ mile of a train track versus 0.03% in Brooklyn. (The five counties also differed in suicide rates by jumping, prescribed medications, trains and subways, methods for which the availability also differed by county.)

FOLLOW-UP STUDIES

O'Donnell et al. (1994) followed-up 94 attempted suicides on the London Underground in 1977-1979 for ten years. Nine had died during the follow-up period of natural causes, and a further nine (10%) were probably suicides (although only seven were classified as suicides by coroners). The time interval between the attempt and the suicide ranged from 1 day to 43 months. Krysinska and De Leo (2008) suggested that this relatively low rate of repetition might be a result of the cathartic impact of surviving a near-lethal suicide attempt.

THE IMPACT OF SUGGESTION AND THE MEDIA

O'Donnell et al. (1994) found that roughly half of those who survived a suicide attempt on the London subway (and, therefore, could be interviewed) knew someone who had completed or attempted suicide using this method (such as fellow psychiatric patients).

Sonneck et al. (1994) studied suicides on the Vienna (Austria) subway which opened in 1978. In the 1980s, the number of suicides rose dramatically (from zero in 1983 to 7 in 1984 and 13 in 1986). The modal suicide was 20-29 (younger than other Viennese suicides) and male. Nonfatal suicide attempts also occurred, primarily by people standing on the tracks rather than falling or laying on the tracks. Attempts were more common in the busier stations, whereas completed suicides showed no such relationship. After June 1985, clusters began to occur, slightly more often involving women. In 1986, all but one subway suicide was reported in the media. The Austrian Association for Suicide Prevention wrote guidelines for the media which were followed by the media. In 1988, no subway suicide was reported by the media. The number of subway suicides declined from 1988 on, averaging 5 per year for 1989-1992 (compared to 13 in 1986).

PREVENTING SUBWAY SUICIDES

Clarke and Poyner (1994) systematically examined ways in which subway suicides might be prevented. They noted first that, in the London Underground, most suicides occurred from the platforms, from the first third of the platform, and by crushing (rather than electrocution). They suggested four tactics.

Reduced Access

Platform barriers would reduce access to the tracks. Barriers could be placed for the first half of the platform since, after the train has reached the second half, it has slowed considerably. As noted above, some new subway systems have walled-in platforms with doors which open to permit access to the trains. To prevent access to the tunnels, ramps leading to the tunnels should have gates. If people do enter these areas, infra-red beams can be used to alert staff (O'Donnell & Farmer, 1992). Some stations have many "through" trains which pass at high speeds and do not stop. These trains could be placed on lines which do not have easy platform access.

Law et al. (2008) used a natural quasi-experiment in the subways in Hong Kong where one system ((MTR) installed platform screen doors (in order to reduce air-conditioning costs, as in Singapore) while the other system (KCR) did not. The doors were installed during the period 2002-2005. On the MTR system, there were 38 suicides in the five-year period 1997-2001 but only 7 in the five-year period 2003-2007. In contrast, the corresponding numbers for the KCR system were 13 and 15, respectively. The reduction in suicides on the MTR system seemed to be present both for those with a psychiatric history and those without such a history. Suicide on the railway did not constitute a large proportion of the suicides in Hong Kong, and so the installation of platform doors did not impact the total Hong Kong suicide rate. In addition, at this time, suicide by using the gas emitted from burning charcoal became very popular for suicide, and the total suicide rate rose in Hong Kong (Liu et al., 2007).

Improved Surveillance

Platforms should have "no-standing" areas at the platform edge clearly marked (and, I might add, brightly painted), and staff should enforce this rule, using closed-circuit television (CCTV) and a public-address system. If people do not respond, the drivers of incoming trains can be alerted.

Gaylord and Lester (1994) studied suicides in the Hong Kong subway and noted that the staff use several cues to detect potential suicides, whereupon they send staff members to intervene:

(1) people who loiter near the entrance tunnel
(2) people who take off their shoes or other items of clothing or who set down bags and packages
(3) people who put down bags as the train approaches
(4) possession of personal items of sentimental value such as stuffed toys, dolls, or framed pictures.
(5) erratic behavior, such as intoxication or over-deliberate movements such as praying.

(6) unusual make-up or disguise such as wearing broad-rimmed hats, or avoiding face-to-face contact.

Staff are dispatched if these cues are observed on the CCTV system. The staff are trained to make indirect approaches (such as simply standing there or asking for an ID card) to avoid startling the person. Staff avoid surprising the suspect and will often remove their hat and start an ordinary conversation. Once rapport has been established, the staff try to move the suspect away from the danger area and then begin to assess the suicide potential of the suspect.

Emergency Stops

CCTV might be made available to train drivers so that they could have advance sighting of the platforms they are about to enter. Some stations on the Victoria Line in the London subway system have emergency buttons on the platform so that staff can stop trains in the tunnel. A third tactic is to slow train speeds as they approach a platform (to about 10 miles per hour). Rubber tires also facilitate braking.

Reducing Injury

There are three methods of reducing injury: (1) suicide pits under the rails in station areas, (2) a three rail system and elimination of the negative rail (which prevents people falling into the pits), and (3) a skirt or air bag placed on the front of trains to prevent bodies from passing under the train.

Research on automobile design and the impact on pedestrian injury support this third method. For example, Robertson (1990) found that cars with sharp front corners resulted in a higher death rate for pedestrians struck by these cars. Chawla et al. (2000) used crash dummies to show that the bumper height on trucks, bumper offset and grill inclination (but not bumper width) had significant effects on the severity of injuries to the dummy, and they concluded that it is possible to make the fronts of vehicles safer for pedestrians. The same might well be possible, therefore, for trains also.

Publicity

Finally, Clarke and Poyner supported the suggestion of Sonneck et al. (1994) for reducing publicity about subway suicides.

DISCUSSION

An important consideration is whether those who use trains and subways for suicide are more psychiatrically disturbed than other suicides. Mishara (1999) examined 129 suicides in the Montreal subway system from 1986 to 1996. Two-thirds had attempted suicide in the past, and 9% had attempted suicide in the subway. One hundred and five of the suicides had psychiatric problems, 73% had had inpatient psychiatric treatment and, at the time of the suicide, 27% were residing in mental health facilities.

Lindekilde and Wang (1985) studied suicides in the Fyn region of Denmark. They found that 81% of the train suicides had received psychiatric treatment in the past compared to only 38% of all other suicides.[1] The fact that several stations on the London Underground near psychiatric hospitals had high rates of subway suicide is suggestive but not conclusive.

With the exception of the study by Law et al. (2008) mentioned above, no study has yet examined changes in the design of subway stations to explore what impact the changes have on suicide rates. As a result, the issue of substitution of methods when one is made less available has not been studied with regard to subway suicides.

On the other hand, the suggestions made for reducing subway suicide appear to have great merit. For example, the fact that subway systems with walled in platforms and sliding doors to permit entrance to trains experience few if any suicides indicates that subway suicides can be prevented by making access to the trains less easily available.

Radbo et al. (2008) proposed a set of prevention tactics for suicides under trains similar to those proposed for subway systems, but suicides under regular trains seem less easy to prevent. For example, it is less feasible to fence in every railway line in a country or to have walls on platforms with doors that match those of a train that stops in the station. However, some of the measures proposed for

---

[1] Other studies of the psychiatric history of train and subway suicides (such as Mishara's) either did not use a comparison group or used data on suicides studied and/or diagnosed by other investigators.

preventing subway suicides may have some application to regular trains - such as systems to warn train drivers of people on the tracks, improved braking systems, and changes in the design of the front of trains and the wheel design (to reduce the danger that the wheels cut objects in their path).

REFERENCES

Baumert, J., Erazo, N., & Ladwig, K. H. (2005). Ten-year incidence and time trends of railway suicides in Germany from 1991 to 2000. *European Journal of Public Health*, 16, 173-178.

Chawla, A., Mohan, D., Sharma, V., & Kajzer, J. (2000). Safer truck front design for pedestrian impacts. *Journal of Crash Prevention & Injury Control*, 2, 33-43.

Clarke, M. (1994). Railway suicide in England and Wales, 1820-1949. *Social Science & Medicine*, 38, 401-407.

Clarke, R. V., & Poyner, B. (1994). Preventing suicide on the London Underground. *Social Science & Medicine*, 38, 443-446.

Coats, T. J., & Walter, D. P. (1999). Effect of station design on death in the London Underground. *British Medical Journal*, 319, 957.

De Leo, D., & Krysinska, K. (2008). Suicidal behaviour by train collision in Queensland, 1990-2004. *Australian & New Zealand Journal of Psychiatry*, 42, 772-779.

Emmerson, B., & Cantor, C. (1993). Train suicides in Brisbane, Australia, 1980-1986. *Crisis*, 14, 90-94.

Farmer, R., O'Donnell, I., & Tranah, T. (1991). Suicide on the London Underground System. *International Journal of Epidemiology*, 1991, 20, 707-711.

French, H. W. (2000). Japanese trains try to shed a gruesome appeal. *New York Times*, June 6, A4.

Gaylord, M. S., & Lester, D. (1994). Suicide in the Hong Kong Subway. *Social Science & Medicine*, 38, 427-430.

Guggenheim, F. G., & Weisman, A. D. (1972). Suicide in the subway. *Journal of Nervous & Mental Disease*, 155, 404-409.

Johnston, D. W. C., & Waddell, J. P. (1984). Death and injury patterns, Toronto Subway System 1954-1980. *Journal of Trauma*, 24, 619-622.

Kerkhof, A. (2003). Railway suicide. *Crisis*, 24, 47-48.

Krysinska, K., & De Leo, D. (2008). Suicide on railway networks. *Australian & New Zealand Journal of Psychiatry*, 42, 763-771.

Law, C. K., Yip, P. S. F., Chan, W. S. C., Fu, K. W., Wong, P. W. C., & Law, Y. W. (2008). Evaluating the effectiveness of barrier installation for preventing railway suicides in Hong Kong. *Journal of Affective Disorders*, in press.

Lester, D. (1995). Subway suicide rates and national suicide rates. *Perceptual & Motor Skills*, 80, 954.

Lindekilde, K., & Wang, A. G. (1985). Train suicide in the county of Fyn 1979-1982. *Acta Psychiatrica Scandinavica*, 72, 150-154.

Liu, K. Y., Beautrais, A., Caine, E., Chan, C., Chao, A., Conwell, Y. Law, C., Lee, D., Li, P., & Yip, P. S. F. (2007). Charcoal burning suicides in Hong Kong and urban Taiwan. *Journal of Epidemiology & Community Health*, 61, 248-253.

Marzuk, P. M., Leon, A. C., Tardiff, K., Morgan, E. B., Stajic, M., & Mann, J. J. (1992). The effect of access to lethal methods of injury on suicide rates. *Archives of General Psychiatry*, 49, 451-458.

Mishara, B. L. (1999). Suicide in the Montreal subway system. *Canadian Journal of Psychiatry*, 44, 690-696.

O'Donnell, I., Arthur, A. J., & Farmer, R. D. J. (1994). A follow-up study of attempted railway suicides. *Social Science & Medicine*, 38, 437-442.

O'Donnell, I., & Farmer, R. D. T. (1992). Suicidal acts on metro systems. *Acta Psychiatrica Scandinavica*, 86, 60-63.

O'Donnell, I., & Farmer, R. D. T. (1994). The epidemiology of suicide on the London Underground. *Social Science & Medicine*, 38, 409-418.

Radbo, H., Svedung, I., & Andersson, R. (2005). Suicides and other fatalities from train-person collisions on Swedish railroads. *Journal of Safety Research*, 423-428.

Radbo, H., Svedung, I., & Andersson, R. (2008). Suicide prevention in railways systems. *Safety Science*, 46, 729-737.

Robertson, L. S. (1990). Car design and risk of pedestrian deaths. *American Journal of Public Health*, 80, 609-610.

Schmidtke, A. (1994). Suicidal behaviour on railways in the FRG. *Social Science & Medicine*, 38, 419-426.

Sonneck, G., Etzerdorfer, E., & Nagel-Kuess, S. (1994). Imitative suicide on the Viennese subway. *Social Science & Medicine*, 38, 453-457.

Symonds, R. L. (1985). Psychiatric aspects of railway suicides. *Psychological Medicine*, 15, 609-621.

Symonds, R. L. (1994). Psychiatric and preventative aspects of rail fatalities. *Social Science & Medicine*, 38, 431-435.

Van Houwelinger, C. A. J., & Kerkhof, A. J. F. M. (2008). Mental healthcare status and psychiatric diagnoses of train suicides. *Journal of Affective Disorders*, 107, 281-284.

Chapter 6

MEDICATIONS AND POISONS

> Sri Lanka has been suffering from a growing epidemic of suicide attempts...fueled by the ready availability of poison from the fruit of a common roadside plant [yellow oleander]....[A]n old man...had fallen out with his wife, over his habit of feeding the neighbourhood dogs. You care more about those dogs than me, said the wife. The man, feeling that his Buddhist principles were under attack, walked out and swallowed a seed from a tree in his garden.
>
> — Jenkins, 2006

Barraclough et al. (1971) noted that 30% of the suicides in England and Wales in 1968 used barbiturates for committing suicide, and barbiturates constituted the most popular drug for committing suicide. Given such figures, it would seem obvious that one tactic for possibly preventing suicide would be to restrict access to medications that can be used for committing suicide. Barraclough and his colleagues suggested:

(1) reducing the number of prescriptions for such medications,

(2) reducing the size of the prescriptions,

(3) wrapping tablets individually in tin foil or plastic blisters,

(4) using non-barbiturates (and other lethal medications) when less lethal medications exist for the same problems,

(5) having family physicians recall unused tablets when the treatment is changed or stopped,

(6) writing prescriptions in a way that would prevent forgery,

(7) having pharmacists monitor large and excessive prescriptions, and

(8) not prescribing medications or refilling prescriptions without seeing the patient.

This chapter explores the possible impact of restricting access to medications and poisons might have on the suicide rate.

MEDICATIONS IN GENERAL

It is difficult to get data on the prescription of medications over time and over regions. Cook (1982) proposed that accidental death rates by be used to indicate the availability of a lethal method for suicide and homicide. For example, Cook used the accidental death rate from firearms in a community as a measure of the availability of firearms in the community. In a series of studies, Lester used the accidental death rates from medications as an index of their availability.

Lester (1990b) found that, in the United States from 1950 to 1984, the accidental death rate for solids and liquids was positively associated with the suicide rate from this method. (This association was also found specifically for barbiturates.) Lester and Abe (1990) replicated this result in Japan for 1950-1980.

Lester also carried out regional studies of these associations. In the United States he found that the accidental death rates from poisoning by solids/liquids (and by gasses too) were positively associated with the suicide rates using these methods over the states of America (Lester, 1985, 1989c, 1993). Lester and Agarwal (1989) found a similar association for deaths using poisons over the regions of India.

Lester (1991) found that the association between suicidal and accidental deaths over time in the United States from 1979 to 1987 was positive and strong for barbiturates and other sedatives and hypnotics, but not for analgesics/antipyretics/antirheumatics or for tranquilizers/other psychotropic agents.

Lester (1994a) used the per capita availability of doctors in European nations as a proxy measure of the prescription rate and found that the measure was positively associated with the suicide rates using solids and liquids, but not with the suicide rate by all other methods. Lester (1994b, 1995) replicated this result over the states of America, but failed to replicate it over regions of Russia.

Many studies have informally documented an association between the rates of prescribing particular medications and their use for attempted and completed suicide: Adelstein and Mardon (1975) for barbiturates in England, Brewer and Farmer (1985) for hypnotics and tranquilizers in England, Ekeberg et al. (1987) for barbiturates in Oslo (Norway), Forster and Frost (1985) for psychotropic drugs in England, McMurray et al. (1987) for distalgesic and mefenamic agents in

Scotland, and Whyte et al. (1989) for a variety of benzodiazepine agents in Australia. However, Ekeberg et al. (1987) and Adelstein and Mardon (1975) both found evidence for switching to other medications. (The other studies did not explore the possibility of switching.) Moens, and van de Voorde (1989) did not find any associations between prescription rates for various medications and the overall suicide rate in Belgium, but they did not look at the suicide rate by solids/liquids specifically.

Ohberg et al. (1995) studied suicide in Finland from 1947-1990. They documented that restrictions of the availability of parathion in 1959 led to a decline its use for suicide, whereas a rise in the prescribing of antidepressants in the 1980s led to an increase in their use, particularly for the tricyclics. (The effect of the decreasing prescribing of barbiturates was ambiguous - the number of suicides using barbiturates declined but the ratio of suicides to prescribed "daily doses" did not.)

Carlsten et al. (1996) studied the association of sales of various medications and their use for suicide in Sweden for the period 1969-1992. The suicide rates for barbiturates, analgesics (paracetamol and dextropropoxyphene) and antidepressants followed the sales curves for these three medications, the curves for barbiturates both decreasing and those for analgesics and antidepressants all increasing. The results for neuroleptics were less clear since sales, and the suicide rate using these medications did not change much.

Sedatives

Oliver and Hetzel (1972) investigated the association between the increased availability of sedatives in Australia and their use for suicide in the period 1955-1970. During that period, the number and percentage of suicides using medications increased both for men and for women. Suicide using other methods showed only small fluctuations. The increase in drug suicides accounted for all of the rise in the Australian rates during this period.

In 1960, sedatives were made more readily available to Australians, and prescriptions for them increased through 1967, along with their use for suicide. In 1967, restrictions on the prescribing of sedatives were introduced. Thereafter, the suicide rate using drugs declined. Oliver and Hetzel noted that the rate of drug suicide and the rate of prescribing sedatives showed similar trends over the period studied. A similar decline in the use of barbiturates was noted in North-West India after restrictions were placed on their over-the-counter sales in 1975 (Singh et al.,

1997), after which there was a large increase in the use of agro-chemicals for suicide, with aluminium phosphide contributing the most to mortality.

In Japan, prior to 1961, barbiturates were available over the counter without a prescription. From February 1st, 1961, the Pharmacy Act S.49 required prescriptions for both barbiturates and meprobamate. Lester and Abe (1989) examined the use of sedative and hypnotics for suicide prior to and after the implementation of this act. The suicide rate using sedatives and hypnotics peaked at 7.05 per 100,000 per year in 1958. Thereafter, the suicide rate using sedatives and hypnotics declined consistently. Thus, at the time when the pharmacy act was implemented in 1961, the suicide rate using sedatives and hypnotics was already declining. The slope of the regression line describing this decline did increase a little after the implementation of the act. The suicide rate by all other methods began declining even earlier, after 1955 in fact, and continued to decline until 1965. Thus, there was no evidence the people switched methods for suicide once prescriptions were required for sedatives and hypnotics.

Barbiturates

In the United States from 1960 to 1974, Lester (1989b, 1990a) found that the suicide rate using barbiturates was associated with the annual sales volume of barbiturates and with the accidental death rate from barbiturates.

Melander et al. (1991) carried out an intervention in Malmo, Sweden. In 1978, Malmo had higher rates of prescribing barbiturates than either Goteborg or Stockholm, and the use of barbiturates for suicide was also greater in Malmo. All the doctors in Malmo were contacted by letter and called to meetings. They were given information about the abuse of barbiturates and encouraged to prescribe smaller amounts, low dosages, and intermittent use. All doctors were informed how their prescribing practices compared to others, and those doctors prescribing higher amounts were personally approached by the head of the Malmo Board of Health.

In the next four years, the prescribing of barbiturates declined in Malmo (by 45%), as did their use for suicide (by 70%). There was no corresponding increase in suicide using other medications or non-pharmacological means, but after about six years, the use of non-pharmacological means for suicide did increase. Thus, switching (or substitution of other methods for suicide) did not occur to any great extent.

In Goteborg, where there was no intervention, prescription rates for sedatives in general increased, as did the overall suicide rate (by all methods). However, the prescribing of barbiturates and their use for suicide also declined (by 34% and 45%, respectively), declines not as high as those in Malmo.

Thioridazine

In 2000, the use of thioridazine was restricted in Great Britain and shortly thereafter was withdrawn by its manufacturer. This resulted in changes in the prescribing practices of antipsychotic medications (Poon et al., 2007). In the Lothian region of Scotland, prescriptions for atypical antipsychotic medications (such as clozapine and risperidone) grew from 2000 to 2003 and then levelled off. In contrast, prescriptions of typical antipsychotics (such as haloperidol and thioridazine) declined from 2000 to 2003 and then levelled off. During this period, the proportion of admissions for poisoning with atypical antipsychotics increased while the proportion with typical antipsychotics decreased. Restricting the sale of the typical antipsychotics, therefore, resulted in a reduction in their use in poisoning. There was an overall reduction in the use of all types of antipsychotics, indicating less than total switching to other medications.

Opiates

Lester (1989a) used data from Clark (1985) to show that, after prescriptions were required for opiates in England in the early 1900s, the use of opiates for suicide declined.

Use of Parents' Medications

Matusevich et al. (2006) studied youths under the age of 21 who overdosed with medications in Buenos Aires, Argentina, of whom 53% had attempted suicide. Of those overdosing with medications, 83% used medications belonging to their parents, mostly psychotropics (93%). This study did not employ any controls (such as comparing the frequency of medications available in the homes of youths attempting suicide and those not making any attempts), and so the role of availability of medications is not proven by this study. However, it does suggest an important area of research for the future.

Fatal Toxicity Indices

There have been many reports comparing the mortality (from accidental and suicidal deaths) of each of the major antidepressants (e.g., Henry, 1997, Morgan et al., 2004). For example, the tricyclic antidepressants had much higher rates of death per million prescriptions (34) than the monoamine oxidase inhibitors (13) and the selective serotonin reuptake inhibitors (2) (Henry, 1997). Thus, it would seem more appropriate to prescribe the less dangerous antidepressants to depressed patients as the first choice.

Does Warning Physicians Have an Impact?

In 1978, the FDA in the United States warned physicians about prescribing propoxyphene (e.g., Darvon) to high risk patients, especially in combination with other medications, and to not refill prescriptions over the telephone. Soumerai et al. (1987) found that these measures had no impact on the use of the medication for overdoses.

PARACETAMOL

In some European countries, paracetamol (acetaminophen, trade name *Tylenol*) has become a popular method for attempting and completing suicide. It does, however, often cause severe liver (and kidney) damage for those who survive overdoses, and it has become a major problem in health care (Farmer, 1994).

Hawton et al. (1996) interviewed 80 attempted suicides who had used paracetamol in Oxford, England, where 48% of all overdoses in 1993 involved paracetamol. In this sample, 66% were women, 40% aged 13-20 and another 40% aged 21-35. On a suicidal intent scale, 21% had low intent, 39% moderate intent, 34% high intent and 6% very high intent. Almost half (48%) had previously attempted suicide, and 29% had previously overdosed using paracetamol.

Seventy percent of the sample used paracetamol only, 20% paracetamol-containing compounds, and 10% both. Twenty five percent took other substances in addition to paracetamol, and 22% drank alcohol. Sixty percent used blister packs of paracetamol, and these individuals *less* often ingested 25 or more tablets.

However, those using blister packs versus loose tablets in a bottle did not differ in suicidal intent or premeditation.

Forty one percent of the sample had obtained the paracetamol less than an hour before ingesting it. Only 20% had contemplated taking the overdose for more than a day. A clinical assessment indicated that only 30% of the sample had wanted to die, 25% did not, and 36% did not care.

Research on Restricting Paracetamol

Gunnell et al. (1997) compared paracetamol overdoses in England and France. In both countries, the rates of attempted and completed suicide using paracetamol rose during the 1980s in parallel as well as with the rate of sales of paracetamol. However, suicide rates using paracetamol were four times higher in England than in France. Gunnell and his colleagues noted that France restricts sales of paracetamol to pharmacists and to 8 g maximum. In contrast, England permitted sales up to 12 g in supermarkets. Hughes et al. (2003) estimated that 70,000 suicide attempts occurred each year, with only about 150 fatal. In France, where the content of packs has been limited to 8 g since the early 1980s, the fatality rate from paracetamol is much less.

In 1998, the British government reduced the number of 500 mg tablets in packets to 16 in regular stores and 32 in pharmacies, limited the number that could be purchased at one time, and required blister packs. Hughes et al. (2003) studied admissions for paracetamol poisoning in two hospitals in Birmingham. Prior to the legislation, 360 people were admitted each year; afterwards only 250. Prior to the legislation, 76 people were admitted to the liver unit after paracetamol overdoses; afterwards 36. Prince et al. (2000) noted a reduction after 1998 in severe paracetamol poisoning in Newcastle (and nationally), while Turvill et al. (2000) noted a reduction in paracetamol overdoses and in severe overdoses in Middlesex (and, as a control, no change in overdoses by benzodiazepines).

Morgan et al. (2007) examined mortality rates from paracetamol poisoning in England and Wales for 1993 to 2004. After the regulations were imposed in 1998, the age-standardized morality rate from paracetamol dropped, from 8.1 per million in 1993 to 5.3 in 2004. However, the mortality from aspirin and antidepressants also dropped, as did mortality from nondrug poisoning. Thus, factors other than the new regulations may have been responsible for the decline in mortality from paracetamol. Commenting on this study, Buckley and Gunnell (2007) noted that the regulations imposed on paracetamol also applied to sales of aspirin, and so the decline in mortality from aspirin was to be expected. Similarly, the decline in mortality from antidepressants may have resulted from changes in their prescription frequency and the use of the newer, less toxic, SSRIs.

Bateman et al. (2006) examined the impact of restricting sales of paracetamol in Scotland in 1998 on deaths and found that the legislation did not have a preventive impact on deaths. In fact, the number of deaths each quarter from paracetamol products increased for both men and women. The number of discharges from hospitals with poisoning from paracetamol fell. However, most of the deaths were from ingestion of co-proxamol (a combination of paracetamol and dextropropoxyphene, an opioid), for which the prescription rate declined only from 1.42 million in 1995 to 1.26 million in 2003. The restrictions affected only over-the-counter sales, not prescribed paracetamol products.

Sandilands and Bateman (2008) noted that, after co-proxamol was withdrawn from the market, beginning in 2005, the number of deaths in Scotland from co-proxamol dropped (from 41 in 2004 to only 10 in 2006). Interestingly, deaths from all poisons also declined (from 173 in 2004 to 128 in 2006). After the withdrawal of co-proxamol, prescriptions for other analgesics (such as cocodamol and paracetamol) increased, but this was not accompanied by an increase in deaths from these medications, which remained roughly the same as before. Thus, switching of medications for suicide does not appear to have occurred, but Sandilands and Bateman did not examine changes in other methods for suicide or the overall suicide rate.

Hughes et al. (2003) noted that chemicals could be added to paracetamol to reduce its toxicity (such as androstanol, a steroid), but this tactic raises financial problems (increasing the cost of the tablets) and ethical problems since it would force people to take a drug that is not desired and may cause harm.

Balit et al. (2002) found no effect of a paracetamol recall in Australia in 2000 (as a result of product tampering) on their use for poisoning (measured by calls to a poison control service and pediatric accidental poisonings, but they did not study not suicidal behavior *per se*) as compared to 1997–1999. However, the recall lasted only brief periods (March 16th to May 21st and June 6th to August 23rd), and such periods of reduced availability may be too brief to have a detectable effect. Measures of self-poisoning by other analgesics, however, did increase during the recall periods.

In Denmark, Ott et al. (1990) found no epidemic of deaths from paracetamol as the sales of paracetamol increased from one million defined daily doses (DDD) per year in 1978 to 47 million DDD in 1986. (Deaths from salicylates increased despite their declining sales!) The numbers of deaths per million DDD in 1986 were 0.07 for paracetamol, 0.23 for salicylates, 8.2 for dextropropoxyphene and 4.9 for opioids. Ott et al. noted that tablets that combined paracetamol with dextropropoxyphene were never sold in Denmark whereas they were in countries such as England, and the absence of the combination tablet may be behind the different impact of increasing paracetamol sales.

A large number of studies of the effects of legislation regarding package size after September 1998 on paracetamol overdoses have appeared from hospital research teams in the United Kingdom. Robinson et al. (2000) in Northern Ireland compared those taking overdoses before and after that date and found a reduction in the total amount ingested and a reduced serum concentration of paracetamol in the attempted suicides. Hawton et al. (2001) combined data from seven hospitals, and found a significant decrease in the number of tablets per overdose, a significant decrease in admissions to liver units, and a significant decrease in deaths, although there was no significant decrease in the number of tablets of paracetamol sold. Thomas and Jowett (20021) in Wales found a reduction in the proportion of overdoses of more than 30 tablets, but they found evidence for switching to other medications.

Fagan and Wannan (1996) suggested that public education about the effects and dangers of paracetamol and dissemination of information might reduce their use for suicide better than reducing pack-size and labeling the actual packages, but they presented no evidence for the effectiveness of this tactic. Hawton et al. (1995) asked attempted suicides who use paracetamol why they chose it. The majority (62%) said they chose it because it was available, 36% because it was dangerous, and 5% because it was cheap. Some 77% thought that their overdose would kill them, and only 20% knew that it could cause permanent liver damage or harm. Thus, they displayed a great deal of ignorance about its effects, but the results were quite different from a similar survey in 1976 (Gazzard et al., 1976) when the majority of respondents thought that it was not a dangerous medication.

Gunnell et al. (2000) surveyed several countries for their experience with paracetamol and concluded that, in countries where paracetamol is more freely available (Denmark, England and Wales, and the United States), fatality rates from paracetamol overdoses are much higher than in countries where sales are restricted (Belgium, France, Germany, Finland, and Switzerland), although Sweden is an exception.

Morgan and Majeed (2005) reviewed research on the impact of restricting paracetamol, primarily in the UK and judged the studies to be methodologically unsound, making the drawing of reliable conclusions difficult. They concluded that the 1998 regulations appeared to have reduced admission to liver units and liver transplants, reduced hospital admissions for paracetamol, and reduced sales of paracetamol. There was no good evidence for a reduction in suicide mortality from paracetamol.

Tactics for Prevention

Gunnell et al. (2000) reviewed many suggestions for reducing the role of paracetamol in overdoses, with their advantages and disadvantages, including: (1) adding methionine to the tablets to reduce the toxic effects (but which may lead to side affects for some people), (2) public education about its dangers (which may instead highlight its possibilities for suicide), (3) warning notices on packets (which may also highlight its possibilities for suicide), (4) using blister packs, (5) restricting sale to pharmacies, (6) making paracetamol available only by prescription, and (7) restricting the quantity which may be purchased at one time. Suggestions (4) through (7) all lead to inconvenience to those who wish to use paracetamol legitimately.

Hawton et al. (1996) interviewed 80 people who overdosed on paracetamol. Of these, 66% said they would take it anyway even if they had known of the dangers, but only 35% would have had they known of the delay in harm (that is, they would not know of the harm for several days). Only 25% thought that a warning on the pack would have deterred them. Only 20% would have overdosed on paracetamol had a prescription been required to obtain it, 31% would still have taken an overdose had paracetamol contained an antidote to prevent harmful effects, and 37% would have taken a smaller overdose or none at all had the number of tablets been limited.

Hawton et al. (1996) concluded that, although making a prescription necessary for purchasing paracetamol and including an antidote might be effective in reducing its use for suicide, both were impractical. Mild analgesics are necessary, and the long-term side effects of the possible antidotes are not yet fully known. Blister-packaging seems to be ineffectual in preventing overdoses, but they did seem to reduce the proportion of serious overdoses (which result in severe liver damage). Highlighting the delay in the effects may also deter some individuals from overdosing with paracetamol. However, Hawton et al. concluded that limiting the number of tablets available in over-the-counter bottles was the most pragmatic tactic for reducing the use of paracetamol for suicidal actions.

PESTICIDES

In recent years, attention has been drawn to the growing use of pesticides and herbicides by those completing and attempting suicide in developing countries, especially in rural areas (Gunnell & Eddleston, 2003). These chemicals are easily available and kept in or close to the farmer's house. Furthermore, in these regions of the world, farmers are numerous, each farming a small plot, as compared to the large-scale farming in developed countries. Phillips et al. (2002) found that 65% of suicides using pesticide in China used chemicals stored in the home. They have become the most common method for suicide in some countries, for example, Trinidad and Tobago (Daisley & Hutchinson, 1998) and in rural regions of India (Chowdhury et al., 2007).

In the world as a whole, Gunnell et al. (2007) estimated that roughly 258,000 suicides occur each year from pesticides, accounting for 30% of suicides globally. This percentage ranged from 4% in Europe to over 50% in the Western Pacific. Gunnell et al. suggested that the use of pesticides for suicide is not determined simply by the sales volume. Europe accounts for 29% of the sales of pesticides but only 2% of the suicides by this method. The use of pesticides is facilitated by the proportion of small-holders and the toxicity of the pesticides used.

Who Uses Pesticides for Suicide?

In one region of southern India from 1986 to 2005, Alex et al. (2007) found that 43% used poisoning (of whom 68% used pesticides), a method used more often by those under the age of 40 and by men. In one region of West Bengal, India, Chowdhary et al. (2007) identified 5187 incidents of deliberate self-harm, 85% of whom used pesticides. Other poisons used included sedatives and homeopathic medicines, household poisons (such as kerosene, rat killers and lice killers) and indigenous poisons (such as oleander seeds).

Research on Prevention

Al-Ragheb and Salhab (1989) noted that, in Jordan after 1980, there was an increased awareness of the dangers of pesticides, a decrease in the importing of toxic pesticides, a ban on the use of parathion, and the use of less persistent pesticides, and a decline in their use for suicide, but they presented no figures to support their opinion.

Bowles (1995) reported data from Western Samoa where paraquat was introduced as a pesticide in 1972. From 1972 to 1988, the trends for paraquat imports, sales of paraquat to the public, and rates of attempted suicide and completed suicide were parallel. All curves peaked in the early 1980s, declined in the mid-1980s, whereupon they all rose toward the end of the 1980s.

Nandi et al. (1979) studied the impact of restricting the sale, purchase and storage of Endrine, a lethal insecticide, in Daspur in West Bengal, India. The restrictions were imposed in October 1976, and so Nandi compared suicides from January to September in the year before and the year after this change. The numbers of suicides using Endrine dropped from 34 to 25, but the total number of suicides barely changed, going from 51 to 50. Thus, switching methods occurred.

Parron et al. (1996) compared suicide in the El Poniente area of Almeria Province in southeastern Spain with suicides in the surrounding areas for 1976-1987. El Poniente has the highest density of greenhouses in the world. The suicide rate in El Poniente was higher than in the surrounding areas and in the province and Spain as a whole. In particular, the suicide rate was higher in the farmers than in those with other occupations, and the higher suicide rate in the area was almost entirely due to suicide from pesticides.

It is remarkable that, given the tremendous increase in concern about (and scholarly articles on) suicide using pesticides, there has been so little evaluation research of prevention programs. In the past, as one pesticide was banned, others took its place as the favored method for suicide. The bans on parathion and methylparathion in the mid 1980s and those of the last of the Class 1 organophosphates (such as monocrotophos) in 1995 resulted in other pesticides taking their place (such as endosulfan), resulting in an increase of completed and attempted suicides with the new products (Manuweera et al., 2008). It is crucial to explore whether changing the availability of particular pesticides simply switches would-be suicides to alternative pesticides and, more importantly, to methods for suicide other than pesticides. Nandi et al. (1979) demonstrated switching of methods for self-poisoning after a ban on one insecticide thirty years ago! It is astounding that so few evaluative studies have been carried out since then. Furthermore, actual experiments could have been conducted, assigning different pesticide practices to different regions in order to examine their impact.

Gunnell et al. (2007) examined trends in suicide rate in Sri Lanka from 1986 to 2005 during which time restrictions on Class I toxicity pesticides were imposed in 1995 and on endosulfan in 1998. These restrictions on the import and sales of these pesticides were accompanied by a decline in the suicide rate using pesticides and a decline in the total suicide rate. Although the use of hanging increased, the increase was not sufficient to offset the huge decline in the suicide rate using pesticides. Gunnell et al. thought that socio-economic factors such as unemployment, alcohol consumption and the civil war did not have an impact on the decline in the suicide rate, but they did not use a multiple regression analysis to test their opinion.

Pesticides and Depression

There is evidence that exposure to some pesticides (such as organophosphate insecticides) increases the incidence of affective disorders and depression (London et al., 2005). The impact on pesticides on suicide may, therefore, also be indirect (by causing depression which in turns results in a higher rate of suicide) as well as direct (using the pesticide for the suicidal act).

Recommendations

Gunnell and Eddleston (2003) suggested several tactics for reducing the use of pesticides for suicide:

(1) Restricting their availability, directly by restricting their import or use, or indirectly by storing them in secure facilities in communities.
    (i) Introducing a "minimum" pesticides list and restricting use to a few, less toxic pesticides (Eddleston et al., 2002).
    (ii) Prohibiting sales of the most toxic pesticides
    (iii) Subsidizing the cost of less toxic pesticides
    (iv) Keeping all pesticides locked up with the keys held by licensed users
    (v) Reducing their use in farming by implementing other methods of pest control
    (vi) Returning unused pesticides to the vendor.
(2) Improving public education about the dangers of pesticide ingestion and better labeling of pesticides.
(3) Reducing the toxicity of pesticides
    (i) adding emetics or antidotes to pesticides
    (ii) making pesticides unpleasant to smell and taste
    (iii) producing less toxic pesticides
(4) Improving the medical management of pesticide poisoning.

The Toxicity of Pesticides
Eddelston et al. (2005) studied 803 patients who had ingested pesticides and found differences in mortality. Mortality was higher for dimethoate and fenthion than with chlorpyrifos. Wilks et al. (2008) reported that a new paraquat formulation devised to reduce toxicity resulted in higher survival rates during a

test in Sri Lanka. Switching to less toxic pesticides, therefore, could improve survival in those who ingest pesticides.

However, Roberts et al. (2003) documented that, as one pesticide was regulated and eventually banned, another pesticide typically takes over as the agent for self-poisoning. After 1991, the import of WHO Class I organophosphates was reduced, and they were banned for routine use in early 1995. The result seemed to be that WHO Class II organophosphates (such as endosulfan) took their place for self-poisoning. Endosulfan was banned in 1998, but by 2000 the number of deaths from pesticides was similar to the level in 1991. Between 1986 and 2000, the number of admissions due to poisoning increased, but the mortality rate declined. Thus, forcing farmers to switch pesticides may have kept the suicide fatality rate using pesticides from rising.

Improvements in Care

Relevant to suggestion (4) above, Kar (2006) found that those who succumbed to death from organophosphate poisoning in one hospital in India were more often male and were older than those who survived and, more importantly, had more severe symptoms of poisoning and a longer interval between the ingestion of the poison and the specific intervention (7.2 hours versus 4.4 hours). The availability of clinics with the capability of intervening would prevent many deaths.

In addition to providing quicker access to medical care, physicians have developed better procedures for treating patients who have ingested pesticides (e.g., Aardema et al. 2008), thereby increasing survival rates.

Safe Storage

Konradsen et al. (2007a, 2007b) noted problems with providing storage boxes to store pesticides safely. In their study in Sri Lanka, they found that the result of providing safe storage boxes increased the proportion of farmers storing the boxes in their homes (from 54% to 98%), and only 84% locked the boxes. Even when locked, the boxes indicated where the pesticides were stored, and two locked boxes were broken into, resulting in one death. However, the percentage of households keeping pesticides safe from children increased from 64% to 89% and for adults from 51% to 66%.

The Impact on Crops

Hruska and Corriols (2002) trained farmers in one region of Nicaragua in pest management so that they could reduce their use of pesticides. As compared to control farmers, the trained farmers used less pesticide and yet made higher net returns. Although Hruska and Corriols did not study the use of pesticides for suicide, their study does show that the use of pesticides can be reduced and, therefore, they can be made relatively less available.

It might be thought that bans on pesticides would reduce agricultural output. Manuweera et al. (2008) studied the impact of bans on particular pesticides in Sri Lanka in 1995 and 1998, resulting in the use of less toxic pesticides, and found no significant changes in agricultural output.

DISCUSSION

The evidence seems to indicate that restricting access to medications and pesticides does reduce their use for suicide. Furthermore, some of the epidemics in suicide found in some countries, such as Western Samoa, seem to parallel increases in the availability of pesticides and fertilizers.

However, the evidence for whether potential suicides switch methods after their preferred method is less available is less clear. Occasional studies find no evidence for switching (e.g., Lester and Abe, 1989) where some studies find evidence for switching (Nandi et al., 1979). Much more research is needed to explore whether switching occurs and, if it does, under what conditions.

It is a great pity that concern about the use of paracetamol in Great Britain did not lead to studies on the effectiveness of restrictions. Restrictions on the number of tablets per package could have been instituted in some regions a year or two earlier than in other regions. A similar time lag could have been tried for blister packaging. Such tactics may have resulted in more persuasive evidence for the impact of the legislation.

The same tactic could be applied to pesticide studies. Some regions could have more toxic pesticides banned while others could be allowed to use them. The same tactic could be used for storage boxes and other techniques for reducing suicides using pesticides.

A final problem here is that much of the research on paracetamol suicides is conducted in Great Britain where the number of "open" verdicts and undetermined deaths is large. Thus, the use of official data on suicides in Great Britain is suspect. The better research examines all suicides, accidental death, and undetermined deaths to identify all possible suicides. Lester (2002) argued that, until Great Britain commits itself to accurate certification of deaths, the use of official British statistics in research on suicide renders the results impossible to interpret meaningfully.

REFERENCES

Aardem, H., Meertens, J. H. J. M., Ligtenberg, J. J. M., Peters-Polman, O. M., Tullerken, J. E.,& Zijlstra, J. G. (2008). Organophosphate pesticide poisoning. *Netherlands Journal of Medicine*, 66(4), 149-153.

Adelstein, A., & Mardon, C. (1975). Suicides, 1961-1974. *Population Trends*, 2(Winter), 13-18.

Alex, R., Prasad, J., Kuruvilla, A, & Jacob, J. S. (2007). Self-poisoning with pesticides in India. *British Journal of Psychiatry*, 190, 274-275.

Al-Ragheb, S. Y. A. & Salhab, A. S. (1989). Pesticide mortality. *American Journal of Forensic Medicine & Pathology*, 10, 221-225.

Balit, C. R., Isbister, G. K., Peat, J., Dawson, A. H., & Whyte, I. M. (2002). Paracetamol recall. *Medical Journal of Australia*, 176, 162-165.

Barraclough, B. M., Nelson, B., Bunch, J., & Sainsbury, P. (1971). Suicide and barbiturate prescribing. *Journal of the Royal College of General Practitioners*, 21, 645-653.

Bateman, D. N., Gorman, D. R., Bain, M., Inglis, J. H. C., House, F. R., & Murphy, D. ((2006). Legislation restricting paracetamol sales and patterns of self-harm and death from paracetamol-containing preparations in Scotland. *British Journal of Clinical Pharmacology*, 62, 573-581.

Bowles, J. R. (1995). Suicide in Western Samoa. In R. F. W. Diekstra, W. Gulbinat, I. Kienhorst & D. de Leo (Eds.) *Preventive strategies on suicide*, pp. 173-206. Leiden, the Netherlands: E. J. Brill.

Brewer, C., & Farmer, R. (1985). Self-poisoning in 1984. *British Medical Journal*, 290, 391.

Buckley, N. A., & Gunnell, D. (2007). Does restricting pack size of paracetamol (acetominophen) reduce suicides? *PloS Medicine*, 4(4), e152.

Carlsten A., Allebeck, P., & Brandt, L. (1996). Are suicide rates in Sweden associated with changes in the prescribing of medicines? *Acta Psychiatrica Scandinavica*, 94, 94-100.

Chowdhary, A. N., Benerjee, S., Brahma, A., & Biswas, M. K. (2007). Pesticide poisoning in nonfatal, deliberate self-harm. *Indian Journal of Psychiatry*, 49, 117-120.

Chowdhury, A. N., Banerjee, S., Brahma, A., & Weiss, M. G. (2007). Pesticide practices and suicide among farmers of the Sundarban region in India. *Food & Nutrition Bulletin*, 28(2), S381-S391.

Clark, M. J. (1985). Suicide by opium and its derivatives in England and Wales. *Psychological Medicine*, 15, 237-242.

Cook, P. J. (1982). The role of firearms in violent crime. In M. E. Wolfgang & N. A. Weiner (Eds.) *Criminal violence*, pp. 236-291. Beverly Hills, CA: Sage.

Daisely, H., & Hutchinson, G. (1998). Paraquat poisoning. *Lancet*, 352, 1393-1394.

Eddleston, M., Eyer, P., Worek, F., Mohamed, F., Senarathna, L., von Meyer, L., Juszczak, E., Hittarage, A., Azhafr, S., Dissanayake, W., Sheriff, M. H. R., Szinicz, L., Dawson, A. H., & Buckley, N. A. (2005). Differences between organophosphorus insecticides in human self-poisoning. *Lancet*, 366, 1452-1459.

Eddleston, M., Karalliedde, L., Buckley, N., Fernando, R., Hutchinson, G., Osbister, G., Konradsen, F., Murray, D., Piola, J. C., Senanayake, N., Sheriff, R., Singh, S., Siwach, S. B., & Smit, L. (2002). Pesticide poisoning in the developing world. *Lancet*, 360, 1163-1167.

Ekeberg, O., Jacobsen, D., Flaaten, B., & Mack, A. (1987). Effect of regulatory withdrawal of drugs and prescription recommendations on the pattern of self-poisoning in Oslo. *Acta Medica Scandinavica*, 221, 483-487.

Fagan, E., & Wannan, G. (1996). Reducing paracetamol overdoes. *British Medical Journal*, 313, 1417-1418.

Farmer, R. D. T. (1994). Suicide and poisons. *Human Psychopharmacology*, 9, S11-S19.

Forster, D., & Frost, C. (1985). Medicinal self-poisoning and prescription frequency. *Acta Psychiatrica Scandinavica*, 71, 567-574.

Gazzard, B. G., Davis, M., Spooner, J., & Williams, R. (1976). Why do people use paracetamol for suicide? *British Medical Journal*, i, 212-213.

Gunnell, D., & Eddleston, M. (2003). Suicide by intentional ingestion of pesticides. *International Journal of Epidemiology*, 32, 902-909.

Gunnell, D., Eddleston, M., Phillips, M. R., & Konradsen, F. (2007a). The global distribution of fatal pesticide self-poisoning. *BMC Public Health*, 7, #357.

Gunnell, D., Fernando, R., Hewagama, M., Priyangika, W. D. D., Konradsen, F., & Eddleston, M. (2007b). The impact of pesticide regulations on suicide in Sri Lanka. *International Journal of Epidemiology*, 36, 1235-1242.

Gunnell, D., Hawton, K., Murray, V., Garnier, R., Bismuth, C., Fagg, J., & Simkin, S. (1997). Use of paracetamol for suicide and non-fatal poisoning in the UK and France. *Journal of Epidemiology & Community Health*, 51, 175-179.

Gunnell, D., Murray, V., & Hawton, K. (2000). Use of paracetamol (acetaminophen) for suicide and nonfatal poisoning. *Suicide & Life-Threatening Behavior*, 30, 313-313-326.

Hawton, K., Townsend, E., Deeks, J., Appleby, L., Gunnell, D., Bennewith, O., & Cooper, J. (2001). Effects of legislation restricting pack sizes of paracetamol on self-poisoning in the United Kingdom. *British Medical Journal*, 322, 1203-1207.

Hawton, K., Ware, C., Mistry, H., Hewitt, J., Kingsbury, S., Roberts, D., & Weitzel, H. (1995). Why patients choose paracetamol for self-poisoning and their knowledge of its dangers. *British Medical Journal*, 310, 164.

Hawton, K., Ware, C., Mistry, H., Hewitt, J., Kingsbury, S., Roberts, D., & Weitzel, H. (1996). Paracetamol self-poisoning. *British Journal of Psychiatry*, 168, 43-48.

Henry, J. A. (1997). Epidemiology and relative toxicity of antidepressant drugs in overdose. *Drug Safety*, 16, 374-390.

Hruska, A. J., & Corriols, M. The impact of training in integrated pest management among Nicaraguan maize farmers. *International Journal of Occupational & Environmental Health*, 2002, 8, 191-200.

Hughes, B., Durran, A., Langford, N. J., & Mutimer, D. (2003). Paracetamol poisoning. *Journal of Clinical Pharmacy & Therapeutics*, 28, 307-310.

Jenkins, J. Poison plant fuels suicide bids. BBC News, 2006, April 10th. news.bbc.uk/1/hi/health/4888840.stm

Kar, N. (2006). Lethality of suicidal organophosphate poisoning in an Indian population. *Annals of General Psychiatry*, 5, #17.

Konradsen, F., Dawson, A. H., Eddleston, M., & Gunnell, D. (2007a). Pesticide self-poisoning. *Lancet*, 369, 169-170.

Konradsen, R., Pieris, R., Weerasinghe, M., van der Hoek, W., Eddelston, M., & Dawson, A. H. (2007b). Community uptake of safe storage boxes to reduce self-poisoning from pesticides in rural Sri Lanka. *BMC Public Health*, 7, #13.

Lester, D. (1985). Accidental deaths as disguised suicides. *Psychological Reports*, 56, 626.

Lester, D. (1989a). Restricting methods for suicide as a means of preventing suicide. *Perceptual & Motor Skills*, 68, 273-274.

Lester, D. (1989b). Barbiturates sales and their use for suicide. *Perceptual & Motor Skills*, 69, 442.

Lester, D. (1989c). Specific agents of accidental and suicidal death. *Sociology & Social Research*, 73, 182-184.

Lester, D. (1990a). The use of prescribed medication for suicide. *International Journal of Risk & Safety in Medicine*, 1, 279-281.

Lester, D. (1990b). Accidental death rates and suicide. *Activitas Nervosa Superior*, 32, 130-131.

Lester, D. (1991. Iatrogenic concerns in the treatment of suicidal patients. *Pharmacology & Toxicology*, 69, 301-302.

Lester, D. (1993). Availability of methods for suicide and suicide rates. *Perceptual & Motor Skills*, 76, 1358.

Lester, D. (1994a). Estimates of prescription rates and the use of medications for suicide. *European Journal of Psychiatry*, 8, 81-83.

Lester, D. (1994b). Estimates of prescription rates and the use of medicaments for suicide. *Pharmacology & Toxicology*, 75, 231-232.

Lester, D. (1995). Medical resources and the prevention of suicide and homicide. *European Journal of Psychiatry*, 9, 97-99.

Lester, D. (2002). The scientific study of suicide requires accurate data. *Crisis*, 23, 133-134.

Lester, D., & Abe, K. (1989). The effect of controls on sedatives and hypnotics and their use for suicide. *Clinical Toxicology*, 27, 299-303.

Lester, D., & Abe, K. (1990). The availability of lethal methods for suicide and the suicide rate. *Stress Medicine*, 6, 275-276.

Lester, D., & Agarwal, K. S. (1989). Accidental death rates as a measure of the availability of a method for suicide. *Perceptual & Motor Skills*, 68, 66.

London, L., Fisher, A. J., Wesseling, C., Mergler, D., & Kromhout, H. (2005). Suicide and exposure to organophosphate insecticides. *American Journal of Industrial Medicine*, 47, 308-321.

Manuweera, G., Eddelston, M., Egodage, S., & Buckley, N. A. (2008). Do targeted bans of insecticides to prevent deaths from self-poisoning result in reduced agricultural output? *Environmental Health Perspectives*, 116, 492-495.

Matusevich, D., Ruiz, M., Vairo, M., Finkelsztein, C., & Job, A. (2007). Adolescents' suicide attempt with their parent's psychtropic medication. *Vertex*, 17(70), 446-451.

McMurray, J. J., Northridge, D. B., Abernethy, V. A., & Lawson, A. A. (1987). Trends in analgesic self-poisoning in West Fife 1971-1985. *Quarterly Journal of Medicine*, 65, 835-843.

Melander, A., Henricson, K., Stenberg, P., Malmvick, J., Sternebring, B., Kaij, L., & Bergdahl, U. (1991). Anxiolytic-hypnotic drugs. *European Journal of Clinical Pharmacology*, 41, 525-529.

Moens, G. F., & van de Voorde, H. (1989). Availability of psychotropic drugs and suicidal self-poisoning mortality in Belgium from 1971-1984. *Acta Psychiatrica Scandinavica*, 79, 444-449.

Morgan, O., Griffiths, C., Baker, A., & Majeed, A. (2004). Fatal toxicity of antidepressants in England and Wales, 1993-2002. *Health Statistics Quarterly*, 23, 18-24.

Morgan, O., Griffiths, C., & Majeed, A. (2007). Interrupted time-series analysis of regulations to reduce paracetamol (acetominophen) poisoning. *PloS Medicine*, 4(4), e105.

Morgan, O., & Majeed, A. (2005). Restricting paracetamol in the United Kingdom to reduce poisoning. *Journal of Public Health*, 27, 12-28.

Nandi, D. N., Muherjee, S. P., Banerjee, G., Ghosh, A., Boral, G. C., Chowdhury, A., & Bose, J. (1979). Is suicide preventable by restricting the availability of lethal agents? *Indian Journal of Psychiatry*, 21, 251-255.

Ohberg, A., Lonnqvist, J., Sarna, S., Vuori, E., & Penttila, A. (1995). Trends and availability of suicide methods in Finland. *British Journal of Psychiatry*, 166, 35-43.

Oliver, R. G., & Hetzel, B. S. (1972). Rise and fall of suicide rates in Australia. *Medical Journal of Australia*, 2, 919-923.

Ott, P., Dalhoff, K., Hansen, P. B., Loft, S., & Poulsen, H. E. (1990). Consumption, overdose and death from analgesics during a period of over-the-counter availability of paracetamol in Denmark. *Journal of Internal Medicine*, 227, 423-428.

Parron, T., Hernandez, A. F., & Villanueva, E. (1996). Increased risk of suicide with exposure to pesticides in an intensive agricultural area. *Forensic Science International*, 79, 53-63.

Phillips, M. R., Yang, G., Zhang, Y., Wang, L., Ji, H., & Zhou, M. (2002). Risk factors for suicide in China. *Lancet*, 360, 1728-1736.

Poon, H., Elliot, V., Bateman, D. N., & Waring, W. S. (2007). Impact of legislative changes on patterns of antipsychotic prescribing and self-poisoning in Scotland. *Journal of Toxicological Sciences*, 32, 1-7.

Prince, M. I., Thomas, S. H. L., James, O. F. W., & Hudson, M. (2000). Reduction in incidence of severe paracetamol poisoning. *Lancet*, 355, 2047-2048.

Roberts, D. M., Karunarathna, A., Buckley, N. A., Manuweera, G., Sheriff, M. H. R., & Eddelston, M. (2003). Influence of pesticide regulation on acute poisoning deaths in Sri Lanka. *Bulletin of the World Health Organization*, 81, 789-798.

Robinson, D., Smith, A. M. J., & Johnston, G. D. (2000). Severity of overdose after restriction of paracetamol availability. *British Medical Journal*, 321, 926-927.

Sandilands, E. A., & Bateman, D. N. (2007). Co-proxamol withdrawal has reduced suicide from drugs in Scotland. *British Journal of Clinical Pharmacology*, 66, 290-293.

Singh, S., Wig, N., Chaudhary, D., Sood, N. K., & Sharma, B. K. (1997). Changing pattern of acute poisoning in adult. *Journal of the Association of Physicians of India*, 45, 194-197.

Soumerai, S. B., Avorn, J., Gortmaker, S., & Hawley, S. (1987). Effect of government and commercial warnings on reducing prescription misuse. *American Journal of Public Health*, 77, 1518-1523.

Thomas, M. R., & Jowett, N. I. (2001). Restriction has not reduced admissions with self-poisoning. *British Medical Journal*, 322, 554.

Turvill, J. L., Burroughs, A. K., & Moore, K. P. (2000). Change in occurrence of paracetamol overdose in UK after introduction of blister packs. *Lancet*, 355, 2048-2049.

Whyte, I., Dawson, A., & Henry, A. (1989). Deliberate self-poisoning. *Medical Journal of Australia*, 150, 726-727.

Wilks, M. F., Fernando, R., Ariyananda, P. L., Eddelston, M., Berry, D. J., Tomenson, J. A., Buckley, N. A., Jayamanne, S., Gunnell, D., & Dawson, A. (2008). Improvement in survival after paraquat ingestion following introduction of a new formulation in Sri Lanka. *PloS Medicine*, 5(2), e49.

Chapter 7

GUN CONTROL IN CANADA

The issue of whether the availability of firearms has an impact on the incidence of murder and suicide has long been debated, often with strong emotions on both sides of the debate. In the past, most of the research on this issue has been carried out on the United States, partly because the differing gun control laws in each of the 50 states provides a "natural experiment" to explore this issue (see Lester, 1984). However, the debate is also contentious in Canada (see Gabor, 2003), and several research studies have been conducted on Canadian data. The aim of the present chapter is to review this research in order to see whether any sound conclusions can be drawn from it.

Chapdelaine and Maurice (1996) noted more than ten years ago that firearms cause more than 1,400 deaths annually in Canada. In Quebec, most deaths from gunshot wounds occur in the home, more often in rural areas than in urban areas, and from legally acquired hunting weapons which are often not stored in safely (in accordance with regulations in effect in Canada since January 1st 1993). However, firearms are also involved in other acts. Of the 12,850 robberies in Quebec in 1992, 4,320 (33%) involved firearms. Firearms are also used for suicide and, although many other methods are available for committing suicide, the mortality from suicidal actions involving firearms is 92% as compared to only 30% for suicidal actions involving drugs.

Miller (1995) estimated that the costs of gunshot wounds in Canada in 1991, using 1993 Canadian dollars, was $6.6 billion—$4.7 billion for suicide and attempted suicide, $1.1 billion for homicides and assaults, and $0.6 billion for unintentional shootings. Of this total amount, $63 million was spend on medical and mental health care and $10 million on public services. Productivity losses accounted for $1.5 billion. The remaining costs represented the value attributed to pain, suffering and lost quality of life.

Canada has passed several gun control laws (Billl C-51 in 1977, Bill C-17 in 1991, and Bill C-68 in 1995), and a number of articles have appeared examining whether the passage of these laws had any impact on the incidence of suicide and murder in Canada and on the choice of method for committing suicide and murder. This chapter will review this research to see whether any definitive conclusions can be drawn from the research. However, I will first briefly review some comparative studies on suicide and homicide in Canada and the United States.

CANADA VERSUS THE UNITED STATES

For the period 1969–1988, suicide rates were higher in Canada than in the United States, whereas homicide rates were higher in the United States than in Canada (Leenaars & Lester, 1994a). Homicide and suicide rates were associated over time in the United States but unrelated in Canada. Furthermore, whereas the relative size of the youth cohort (ages 15-24) in the United States was associated with the suicide and homicide rates of this cohort, there was no similar association in Canada. Leenaars and Lester (1992) showed that the patterns of suicide rates by age and by sex also differed in the two countries for the period 1960-1988. For example, Canada experienced a much greater increase in the suicide rates of young men than did the United States in the period 1960 to 1988.

Lester (1990) reported that, in 1980, 37.8% of homicides in Canada were committed with guns compared to 64.8% of homicides in the United States. The suicide rates in 1980 for Canada by gun and by all other methods were 4.66 and 9.30 per 100,000 per year, respectively, and for the United States 6.76 and 5.04.

Finley et al. (2008) looked at all of the reported firearm injuries in Canada from 1999-2003 that were treated in trauma centers. Of the 784 incidents, 39.8% were fatal. About 28% of the incidents were suicide attempts, 60% assaults, 6% accidental and 6% unclassified. Men accounted for 94% of the incidents. Assaults were more common in young men and suicidal incidents in older adults. Death was predicted by the injury severity score, age over 45, non-accidental, and occurring at home.

Quan and Arboleda-Florez (1999) found that, in British Columbia in 1984-1995, 43.8% of men over the age of 55 used guns for completing suicide as compared to only 3.7% of women (for whom poisoning was the most common method for suicide).

Lester and Leenaars (1998) argued that there was a subculture of violence in Canada in 1975-1985 by showing that the suicide, homicide and accidental heath rates using guns in the Canadian provinces were all strongly associated. Provinces that a high firearm death rate from one cause also had high firearm death rates from the other two causes.

Sloan et al. (1988, 1990) compared suicide and homicide in Vancouver in Canada and Seattle in the United States, cities of roughly the same size. The suicide rates were of similar magnitude—15.55 per 100,000 per year and 15.12 in Vancouver and Seattle, respectively. Although the rate of suicide by firearm was lower in Vancouver than in Seattle (2.87 versus 6.73), the suicide rate by all other methods was higher in Vancouver than in Seattle (12.68 and 8.39, respectively). The higher homicide rate in Seattle than in Vancouver (11.3 versus 6.9) was mostly accounted for by the higher firearm homicide rate in Seattle than in Vancouver (4.8 versus 1.0). Similarly, the higher rate of aggravated assault in Seattle than in Vancouver (486 versus 420) was mostly accounted for the higher rate using firearms (88 versus 11).

Mauser (1990; Mauser & Margolis, 1992) compared the attitudes of Canadians and Americans toward guns in the 1970s and 1980s. The citizens of both nations favored gun control legislation but also their right to own guns. The primary reason for gun ownership in both countries was for hunting. However, Canadians were more in favor of stricter gun control laws such as the registration of guns (83% versus 67% in Canada and the United States, respectively) and the banning of pistols and revolvers (81% and 45%). About the same proportion of households in both countries possess rifles, and the majority in both nations felt that store owners were justified in using guns to protect their stores in some circumstances. The predictors of support for gun control laws were similar in the two countries. In Canada, support was associated positively with the perception of the effectiveness of gun control laws and living in rural areas and negatively with being male and gun ownership. In America, support was associated in a similar fashion with these variables with one exception—rural living was no longer associated with support for gun control.

Mauser (1996) compared surveys of Canadian and American household around the year 1990 that inquired about the defensive use of firearms and reported that 3.1% of Canadians and 4.1% of American had used firearms against human and animal threats in the prior five years. For human threats alone, the percentages were 1.6% and 3.9% for Canada and the United States, respectively.

Mauser commented that the percentages for Canada were higher than many had believed.

GUN AVAILABILITY IN CANADA

Chapdelaine et al. (1991) reported data from a government-sponsored poll of over 10,000 Canadian households published in 1991. There were an estimated 5.9 million firearms privately owned in 2.2 million households. Of these firearms, 51% were rifles (24% semi-automatic), 39% shotguns (17% semi-automatic), 7% handguns and 3% "other". Thr purpose of ownership was 67% hunting, 13% collecting, 12% target shooting, 2% employment, 1% for self-protection, and 5% unknown.

Men accounted for 85% of the firearm owners, and 45% of the households with at least one firearm had an income over $40,000 and 11% less than $20,000 (as compared with 17% of the Canadian population). No household member had received instruction in the safe care and handling or firearms in the prior 5 years in 51% of the households, and 50% of the households had not used the firearm in the past year.

PROXY MEASURES OF GUN AVAILABILITY

Suicide

Cook (1982) poposed that the percentage of suicides or homicides using firearms could be used as an indirect measure of gun availability, as could the accidental death rate from firearms. In a study of the Canadian provinces in 1980, Lester (1994) found that the accidental death rate from firearms was positively associated with the suicide rate using firearms and to the proportion of suicides using firearms, but negatively to the suicide rate by all other methods. Thus, gun availability did appear to be associated with the use of guns for suicide. However, the percentage of homicides using firearms did not show these same associations.

Lester (2000b) examined changes in the suicide rate in Canada for 1970-1995. Lester used the percentage of suicides plus homicides using guns as a proxy measure of gun availability. This measure was positively associated with the firearm suicide rate and negatively with the suicide rate by all other methods. It was not significantly associated with the total suicide rate. These results indicate that switching of methods for suicide may have occurred when guns were relatively less available.

Lester also used the accidental firearm death rate as a proxy measure of gun availability. This measure was not significantly associated with the firearm suicide rate but was negatively associated with the suicide rate by all other methods and with the total suicide rate. The results from the two proxy measures clearly contradict each other.

Lester (2001) reported that, for 1970–1995, the accidental firearm mortality rate was associated with the percentage of suicides using firearms for the total population, men and women, and for all age groups except those aged 55+. Bridges (2002) extended Lester's analysis for the period 1970–1998 and replicated his results.

Bridges and Kunselman (2004) examined a different time period (1974–1999) and compared the results using homicide versus murder rates. The accidental firearm death rate was positively associated with the suicide rate by firearms and negatively with the suicide rate by all other methods (and not significantly associated with the overall suicide rate). Similar results were obtained for the percentage of suicides and homicide by gun and the percentage of suicides and murders by gun. For this time period, the evidence for switching was stronger than that in Lester's studies.

For Quebec, Simon et al. (1996) used the number of hunting licenses issued in each region as a proxy measure of gun availability. They found a large, positive association between the number of licenses issued in each region and the firearm suicide rate. They also found a strong association between the firearm suicide rate and the overall suicide rate.

Carrington and Moyer (1994b) looked at suicide rates in the Canadian provinces for three years (1987–1989), providing a panel data-set.[1] They used data (for one year) on the percentage of households owning guns (obtained from household surveys) and the percent urbanized in both correlational and regression analyses. They found that gun ownership predicted the firearm suicide rate and the overall suicide rate but not the suicide rate by all other methods. In contrast, urbanization predicted the suicide rate by all other methods and the overall suicide rate, but not the firearm suicide rate. Carrington and Moyer concluded that firearm availability was associated with a higher use of guns for suicide with no evidence of switching methods.

---

[1] This technique simply increased the sample size by a factor of three, resulting in significant associations whereas the associations might not have been significant if data from a single year had been used.

Homicide

Lester (2000b) examined changes in the homicide rate in Canada for 1970–1995. The accidental firearm death rate was positively associated with the firearm homicide rate and negatively with the homicide rate by all other methods. The total homicide rate was not associated with the accidental firearm mortality rate. These results indicate that switching of methods was taking place.

Lester also used the percentage of suicides plus homicides using guns as a proxy measure of gun availability. This measure was positively associated with the firearm homicide rate and the total homicide rate but not with the homicide rate by all other methods. These results indicate that switching of methods did not occur. The results from the two proxy measures clearly contradict each other.

Lester (2001) reported that, for 1970–1995, the accidental firearm mortality rate was associated with the percentage of homicides using firearms for the total population, men and women, and for all age groups except those aged 55+. Bridges (2002) extended Lester's analysis for the period 1970–1998 and replicated his results.

Bridges and Kunselman (2004) examined a different time period (1974–1999) and compared the results using homicide versus murder rates. The accidental firearm death rate was positively associated with the homicide and the murder rates by firearms and the overall homicide and murder rates. The accidental firearm death rate was also positively associated with the homicide and murder rates by all other methods, but not significantly. Similar results were obtained using the proxy measures of the percentage of suicides and homicide by firearm and the percentage of suicides and murders by gun. These results provide no evidence for switching methods.

Armed Robbery

Lester (2000a) looked at robbery rates in Canada for 1974–1995. Using the accidental death rate from firearms as a proxy measure of gun availability, Lester found that this measure was positively associated with the robbery rate using firearms and negatively associated with the robbery rates with other weapons and with no weapons. The same pattern was found using the percentages of suicides plus homicides by gun as a proxy measure of gun availability. Lester concluded that gun availability was associated with robbers switching to guns for their crimes, weapons which have a greater probability of resulting in death to the robbery victims.

Bill C-51 was passed during this period. The two proxy measure of gun availability were strongly associated with each other (r = 0.91) and negatively with the year, indicating that guns became less available over this time period. The robbery rate by firearms declined over the period, while the robbery rates with other weapons and with no weapon increased.

Accidental Deaths

Gabor et al. (2001) found a strong association between measures of gun availability as measured by household surveys in the Canadian provinces and territories in 1988-1997 and the mortality rate from unintentional firearms deaths.

BILL C-51

Centerwall (1991) compared Canadian provinces and American states that are close to the border between the two countries, such as Manitoba and Minnesota. He noted that estimates of handgun ownership in America were 4 to 10 higher than in Canada, while ownership of long guns was similar in two sets of regions. Murder rates were similar in the two sets of regions, but the murder rate using handguns was much higher in the American states than in the Canadian provinces. Centerwall concluded that, "In the relative absence of handguns, dangerously violent Canadians commit their assaults using other mean which are, on the average, as lethal as handguns" (p. 1259).

Sproule and Kennett (1989) noted that gun control laws were stricter in Canada than in the United States. Infractions were federal offenses, whereas each state in the United States has its own laws. Gun control laws can be by-passed in the United States by driving to a state with weak gun controls laws. In addition, handguns are more severely regulated in Canada, being available only to police and security personnel, members of bonafide gun clubs and bonafide gun collectors. Although demonstrating a need for protection is a possible reason for a permit, it is rarely, if ever, granted. For the period 1977 to 1983, the murder rates per 100,000 per year were:

	Handguns	Other Guns	Other Methods
Canada	0.28	0.67	1.79
USA	4.05	1.32	3.31

It can be seen clearly that handguns were used proportionately more often for murder in the United States than in Canada.

Sproule and Kennett (1988) noted that the Canadian parliament introduced stricter a gun control law in 1977 (Bill C-51), which was implemented fully in 1979, and abolished the death penalty at the same time. Sproule and Kennett compared homicide rates in 1972-1976 and 1977-1982. The overall homicide rate did not change significantly, but the homicide rate using firearms did decline from the first to the second time period. They also noted that the average number of victims per murder was greater in both time periods when the murderer used a gun.

Mundt (1990) also studied the impact of Bill C-51. Bill C-51 mandated the purchase of a certificate for buying any gun, strengthened the registration requirements for handguns and other restricted weapons already imposed in 1968, prohibited automatic weapons and sawed-off shotguns and rifles, and imposed mandatory prohibitions on serious criminals. Mundt carried out no statistical analysis but merely provided graphs of firearm incidents in Canada and the United States: (1) Homicide trends in Canada showed no trend from 1974 to 1987; (2) the percentage of homicides using guns in general and handguns declined from 1974 on; (3) there were no clear trends in the rate of armed robbery, although the percentage of armed robberies declined; (4) both the total suicide rate and the suicide rate using firearms declined after 1979; and (5) the accidental death rate from firearms declined from 1974 on. The conclusion is that the decreased use of guns for seems to have been apparent from 1974 on, and did not change noticeably after 1979. However, as mentioned above, Mundt carried out no statistical tests on the data.

Hung 1993) pointed out factual inaccuracies, logical inconsistencies and methodological fallacies in Mundt's article but did not perform any statistical tests of the data. Lester and Leenaars (1994) also commented on Mundt's article, but for the first time presented data and statistical tests. Their study, and their subsequent studies, will be discussed in the next section.

However, before moving on, it is important to note that gun legislation was passed in Canada in 1968, and this legislation may already have had impact on the use of guns for suicide and murder prior to the passage of Bill C-51 in 1977.

Lester and Leenaars have carried out a series of studies on the impact of Bill C-51 on suicide, homicide and accidental death rates in Canada, and the data on which they base their studies are shown in Table 7.1. These data were calculated from raw data obtained from Statistics Canada. The results of the statistical analyses by Leenaars and Lester are also shown in Table 7.1.

Table 7.1. Suicide, homicide and accidental death rates in Canada

	Suicide Total	Guns	Other Methods	% by Gun	Homicide Total	Guns	Other Methods	% by Gun	Accidental Death Rate by Gun
1969	10.91	3.57	7.34	32.7	1.79	0.74	1.04	41.6	
1970	11.33	3.74	7.59	33.0	1.98	0.86	1.12	43.7	0.606
1971	11.86	4.28	7.58	36.1	2.12	0.88	1.24	41.5	0.663
1972	12.19	4.29	7.90	35.2	2.32	0.93	1.39	40.2	0.468
1973	12.58	4.31	8.27	34.3	2.40	1.20	1.43	40.8	0.558
1974	12.98	4.57	8.41	35.2	2.43	1.16	1.23	49.5	0.546
1975	12.37	4.64	7.73	37.5	2.66	0.96	1.50	43.5	0.489
1976	12.76	4.76	8.00	37.3	2.42	1.10	1.46	39.6	0.387
mean	12.12	4.27	7.85	35.2	2.26	0.96	1.30	42.6	
SD	0.72	0.42	0.42	1.8	0.28	0.15	0.17	3.2	
b	0.26*	0.16*	0.10	0.61*	0.10*	0.05*	0.06*	0.11	
1977	14.26	5.46	8.80	38.3	2.57	0.98	1.58	38.4	0.430
1978	14.80	5.48	9.32	37.0	2.43	0.98	1.45	40.2	0.383
1979	14.18	4.65	9.53	32.8	2.46	0.79	1.67	32.2	0.300
1980	14.03	4.68	9.35	33.4	2.07	0.78	1.29	37.8	0.309
1981	13.98	4.81	9.17	34.4	2.30	0.75	1.55	32.7	0.253
1982	14.30	4.88	9.42	34.1	2.42	0.86	1.56	35.7	0.227
1983	15.09	4.97	10.12	33.0	2.38	0.80	1.58	33.6	0.165

Table 7.1. Suicide, homicide and accidental death rates in Canada

	Suicide Total	Guns	Other Methods	% by Gun	Homicide Total	Guns	Other Methods	% by Gun	Accidental Death Rate by Gun
1984	13.69	4.19	9.05	30.6	2.31	0.86	1.45	37.3	0.239
1985	12.85	4.10	8.75	31.9	2.12	0.71	1.41	33.3	0.248
mean	14.11	4.72	9.40	33.4	2.31	0.82	1.49	35.3	
SD	0.68	0.44	0.38	1.9	0.15	0.08	0.12	3.0	
b	-0.15	-0.13*	-0.02	-0.57*	-0.02	-0.02	-0.01	-0.39	
t before/after	5.70*	2.09*	4.81*	1.91	0.41	2.38*	2.66*	4.79*	
1986	14.50	4.69	9.81	32.3	2.17	0.67	1.50		0.198
1987	14.03	4.39	9.63	31.3	2.42	0.75	1.67		0.234
1988	13.05	3.97	9.08	30.4	2.14	0.63	1.51		0.223
1989	12.75	3.93	8.82	30.9	2.40	0.80	1.60		0.281
1990	12.16	3.79	8.37	31.2	2.37	0.71	1.66		0.237
1991	12.78	3.94	8.83	30.8	2.69	0.96	1.73		0.235
1992	12.99	3.67	9.32		2.56	0.87	1.69		0.221
1993	13.14	3.64	9.50		2.17	0.67	1.50		0.152
1994	12.82	3.33	9.49		2.04	0.67	1.37		0.130
1995	13.41	3.08	10.33		1.99	0.59	1.40		0.166

* Significant at the 5% level or better.

Males	Suicide Total	Guns	Other Methods	% by Gun	Homicide Total	Guns	Other Methods	% by Gun	Accidental Death Rate by Gun
1969	15.58	6.50	9.08	41.7	2.42	1.10	1.32	45.6	1.130
1970	16.23	6.73	9.50	41.5	2.45	1.24	1.21	50.6	1.115
1971	17.29	7.85	9.44	45.4	2.77	1.20	1.57	43.5	1.213
1972	17.43	7.92	9.51	45.4	2.94	1.30	1.64	44.2	0.862
1973	18.03	8.01	10.02	44.4	3.09	1.35	1.74	43.8	1.008
1974	18.85	8.39	10.46	44.5	3.06	1.68	1.38	55.0	1.022
1975	17.94	8.56	9.38	47.7	3.53	1.63	1.90	46.1	0.875
1976	18.41	8.79	9.62	47.7	3.21	1.40	1.81	43.6	0.690
mean	17.47	7.84	9.63	44.79	2.93	1.36	1.57	46.55	0.989
SD	1.10	0.83	0.43	2.33	0.38	0.20	0.25	4.14	0.172
b	0.40*	0.32*	0.08	0.82*	0.14*	0.07*	0.08*	-0.03	-0.56*
1977	21.25	10.09	11.16	47.5	3.45	1.45	2.00	42.1	0.743
1978	22.36	9.96	12.40	44.6	3.33	1.43	1.90	42.9	0.651
1979	21.42	8.70	12.72	40.6	3.20	1.14	2.06	35.5	0.544
1980	21.32	8.69	12.63	40.8	2.78	1.12	1.66	40.2	0.580
1981	21.30	8.95	12.35	42.0	2.87	1.04	1.83	36.4	0.447
1982	22.33	9.05	13.28	40.5	3.26	1.22	2.04	37.4	0.418

[1] These means are for the period 1978–1985.

Males	Suicide Total	Guns	Other Methods	% by Gun	Homicide Total	Guns	Other Methods	% by Gun	Accidental Death Rate by Gun
1983	23.41	9.37	14.04	40.0	3.12	1.13	1.99	36.2	0.308
1984	21.40	7.89	13.51	36.9	3.18	1.31	1.87	41.2	0.434
1985	20.46	7.74	12.72	37.8	2.71	1.00	1.71	36.8	0.478
mean	21.75	8.79	12.94	40.4	3.06	1.17	1.88	38.32	0.482
SD	0.91	0.73	0.61	2.38	0.24	0.14	0.15	2.73	0.107
b	-0.07	-0.21	0.14	-0.83*	-0.04	-0.02	-0.01	-0.30	-0.31*
t before/after	8.50*	2.44*	12.60*	3.72*	0.78	2.16*	3.06*	4.69*	7.09*

Females	Suicide Total	Guns	Other Methods	% by Gun	Homicide Total	Guns	Other Methods	% by Gun	Accidental Death Rate by Gun
1969	6.21	0.62	5.59	10	1.15	0.38	0.77	33.3	0.134
1970	6.41	0.73	5.68	11.5	1.50	0.49	1.01	32.5	0.094
1971	6.43	0.71	5.72	11.1	1.48	0.56	0.92	37.7	0.111
1972	6.94	0.66	6.28	9.5	1.69	0.56	1.13	33.2	0.073
1973	7.14	0.62	6.52	8.6	1.71	0.58	1.13	33.9	0.109
1974	7.13	0.76	6.37	10.6	1.79	0.72	1.07	40.3	0.071
1975	6.83	0.73	6.10	10.8	1.80	0.69	1.11	38.5	0.105
1976	7.16	0.77	6.39	10.8	1.63	0.52	1.12	31.7	0.087

mean	6.78	0.70	6.08	10.36	1.59	0.56	1.03	35.14	0.098
SD	0.38	0.06	0.37	0.95	0.22	0.11	0.13	3.21	0.021
b	0.13*	0.01	0.12*	-0.01	0.07*	0.03	0.04*	0.32	-0.04
1977	7.34	0.88	6.46	12.0	1.69	0.52	1.17	30.8	0.120
1978	7.33	1.05	6.28	14.3	1.53	0.53	1.00	34.3	0.119
1979	7.02	0.64	6.38	9.1	1.73	0.45	1.28	26.2	0.059
1980	6.84	0.73	6.11	10.7	1.36	0.45	0.91	32.9	0.041
1981	6.79	0.75	6.04	11.0	1.74	0.46	1.28	26.6	0.065
1982	6.41	0.78	5.63	12.2	1.56	0.51	1.05	33.0	0.040
1983	6.92	0.66	6.26	9.5	1.65	0.48	1.17	29.0	0.024
1984	6.14	0.56	5.58	9.1	1.45	0.42	1.03	28.8	0.047
1985	5.41	0.54	4.87	10.0	1.54	0.42	1.12	27.4	0.023
mean	6.61	0.71	5.89	10.74	1.57	0.46	1.10	29.77	0.052
SD	0.60	0.16	0.51	1.79	0.13	0.04	0.13	3.18	0.031
b	-0.21*	-0.05*	-0.16*	-0.39	-0.01	-0.01	0.01	-0.48	-0.10*
t before/after	0.69	0.23	0.85	0.52	0.28	2.40*	1.11	3.36*	3.47*

Suicide

Lester and Leenaars (1993, 1994) they noted that, in 1969-1976, prior to the passage of Bill C-51, the suicide rate by firearms was increasing (the unstandardized regression coefficient [b] was +0.16, p = .0003), as were the total suicide rate (b=0.26, p = .003) and the proportion of suicides using guns (b=0.61, p = .01). The suicide rate by all other methods did not change significantly (b = 0.10, p > .05).

For the eight years after the passage of Bill C-51, 1978-1985, the suicide rate by firearms decreased (b = -0.13, p = .04), as did the percentage of suicides using firearms (b = -0.57, p = .03), while the suicide rate by all other methods did not change significantly (b = -0.02, p > .05), nor did the total suicide (b = -0.15, p > .05). Lester and Leenaars concluded that Bill C-51 was followed by a decrease in the use of guns for suicide without there being any increase in suicide by all other methods. Substitution of method (or switching) did not occur. The data showed that the effect persisted into the period 1986–1991

Leenaars and Lester (1996) noted that the total suicide rate increased from the period 1969-1976 to the period 1978–1985, as did the suicide rate by all other methods. The suicide rate by firearms increased, but not significantly, while the percentage of suicides using firearms decreased, but not significantly. Thus, the passage of Bill C-51 seems to have lessened the increasing suicide rate by guns in Canada.

Leenaars and Lester (1996) looked at these effects by sex. Looking at the results, for men, suicide rates rose by firearms and by all other methods after the passage of Bill C-51. Thus, this seems to have been a period of increasing suicide rates for men. However, the percentage of men using guns for suicide decreased after the passage of Bill C-51, and the regression coefficients indicated that the use of guns for suicide for 1978–1985 stopped increasing in the way that it had been in the period 1969–1976.

For women, there were no changes in the suicide rates by firearms and by all other methods after the passage of Bill C-51. After 1978, the suicide rates by firearms and by all other methods both began to decrease (as seen from the regression coefficients), and so this seems to have been a period of decreasing suicide rates for women. In summary, for suicide, the passage of Bill C-51 seems to have led men to switch from firearms as a method for suicide to the use of other methods but to have no impact on women.

Leenaars and Lester (1997b) looked at the impact of Bill C-51 by age. The firearm suicide rate decreased after passage of Bill C-51 only for suicides aged 35–64; the firearm suicide rate increased for those aged 15–34 and over the age of

65. The percentage of suicides using firearms declined only for those aged 15–64 while it increased for those over the age of 65. Switching to other methods for suicide was apparent in those aged 15-34 and those over the age of 75. The change in linear trends in the two periods (1969–1976 and 1978–1985) from an increasing trend prior to the passage of the bill to a declining trend after passage of the bill was apparent for those aged 15–44.

Carrington (1999), commenting on an earlier report by Leenaars and Lester (1996) looked at the slopes of the regression lines before and after the passage of Bill C-51, for suicide and for homicide and for both combined and for males and females separately. Most of the trends prior to the passage of Bill C-51 were positive (increasing rates) and statistically significant. Afterwards, most of the slopes were negative and the changes were significant. For both men and women, there was no evidence for switching methods.

During this time period, many social changes were taking place in Canada aside from changes in gun control laws. Leenaars et al. (2003; Leenaars & Lester, 1999) ran multiple regressions for the period 1969-1985 using the passage of Bill C-51 (as a dichotomous variable—before versus after), the percentage of young men aged 15-24, the birth rate, the marriage rate, the divorce rate, the unemployment rate and the median family income to predict the suicide rates overall and for males and for females. In full multiple regressions, Bill C-51 had a significant beneficial impact on the firearm suicide rate overall and for both men and women. A similar beneficial impact was found for the percentage of suicides using firearms. The suicide rate by all other methods increased significantly for men but declined (non-significantly) for women. The total suicide rate declined for women (non-significantly) and increased (significantly) for men. Thus, switching appears to have occurred for men, but not for women.

Lester et al. (2003) noted that an alternative method of statistical analysis (other than comparing pre- and post-periods after a change) is to use an interrupted time-series analysis. This analysis for the period 1969–1985 indicated that the passage of Bill C-51 had no impact on the total suicide rate, but the upward trend in the total suicide rate was less steep after the passage of the Bill. Similar results were obtained for the firearm suicide rate. For both the total suicide rate and the firearm suicide rate, these trends were greater for men than for women. The data for suicide by all other methods showed evidence of displacement for men but not for women.

Bridges (2004) explored the impact of two later gun control laws, Bill C-17 (passed in 1991) and Bill C-68 (passed in 1995) on the suicide rate, using the same technique as Leenaars and Lester. Bill C-17 banned semi-automatic firearms that could be converted to full automatic fire, raised the requirements for screening to obtain a certificate to purchase a firearm, mandated safe storage policies, and banned large-capacity magazines; Bill C-68 required a license to own and to purchase a firearm and to purchase ammunition, banned semi-automatic military assault weapons, as well as short-barreled and small caliber handguns (Cukier, 2000).

Bridges compared the time periods 1984-1990 and 1991-1998. After 1990, the suicide rate by firearms and the percentage of suicides using firearms decreased significantly, whereas the suicide rate by all other methods increased significantly, leaving the overall suicide rate unchanged. After 1990, the suicide rate by firearms and the percentage of suicides using firearms showed a steady, significant decline. These results suggest that the reduced availability of guns led potential suicides to choose other methods for suicide (that is, switching occurred).

Provincial Suicide Rates

Rich et al. (1990) examined the impact on Bill C-51 on suicides in Ontario as a whole and in Toronto Ontario, comparing the periods 1973–1978 and 1979–1983. They found no change in the overall suicide rate in Ontario or in Toronto. There was a significant decrease in the proportion of male suicides using guns in Toronto. (Too few women used guns for the analysis to be meaningful.)

Carrington and Moyer (1994a) compared the periods of 1973–1977 and 1979–1983 as well as 1965–1977 and 1979–1989. They used both crude and age-standardized suicide rates whereas Rich et al. used crude suicide rates. They confirmed that the overall suicide rate in Ontario did not change from the first to the second period. However, looking at trends in the before and after periods, they found that, before the passage of Bill C-51, the overall suicide rate, the firearm suicide rate and the suicide rate using other methods were both increasing. After passage of the bill, all three suicides rates showed a declining trend. The use of age-standardized rates gave results similar to those for crude suicide rates. The fact that suicide by methods other than firearms showed a declining trend after the passage of the bill suggests that there were societal changes other than the passage of the bill that may have led to this declining trend.

Carrington and Moyer (1994b) carried out an analysis similar to those conducted by Leenaars and Lester, using the periods 1965-1977 and 1979-1989 for Canada as a whole and for each province. Nine of the ten Canadian provinces had significantly increasing trends in firearm suicide rates and the total suicide rate for 1965-1977. After the passage of Bill C-51, all ten provinces had either stable or decreasing firearm suicide rates and total suicide rates. None of the provinces had a significant increase in the suicide rate by all other methods for 1979-1989, and so switching methods did not occur.

Caron (2004) examined the impact of the implementation of Bill C-17 in 1992 in the Abitibi-Temiscamingue region of Quebec. While the firearm suicide rate decreased significantly, the suicide rate by all other methods and the overall suicide rate both increased. These trends were found for both men and women. The decrease in the firearms suicide rate was not, however, found for men over the age of 45. Caron concluded that switching of methods occurred to hanging for young adults and to poisoning for women.

Caron et al. (2008) carried out a detailed analysis of suicide rates by method in Quebec for the period 1987-2001, spanning the passage of Bill C-17. Caron et al. examined the periods before and after Bill C-17 was implemented beginning in 1992, looked at trends in the suicide rates before and after 1992, carried out an interrupted time-series analysis, and examined the results of a multivariate regression analysis including divorce and unemployment rates. Their conclusion was that firearm suicide rates decreased after 1992, whereas the overall suicide rate and the suicide rate by all other methods increased, both for the total population and for men and women separately. However, a decreasing trend in firearm suicide rates was apparent prior to 1992, and so the decreasing trend afterwards appears to have been part of this long-term trend and not a result of the passage of Bill C-17. Caron et al. concluded that the passage of Bill C-17 had no impact on the firearm suicide rate in Quebec. The passage of Bill C-17 also appeared to have no impact on the increasing trends in the overall suicide rate or the suicide rate by all other methods in Quebec.

Homicide

It must be noted that the rates and percentages in this section are based on data from victims of homicide, not murderers.

Leenaars and Lester (1994b, 1996, 1997a, 1997b, 2001) examined the homicide rate in Canada before and after the passage of Bill C-51. Leenaars and Lester (1994b) found that the total homicide rate did not change from 1969–1976 to 1978–1985, but the homicide rate by firearms decreased significantly, as did the percentage of homicide using firearms, while the homicide rate using all other methods increased significantly. Since the total homicide rate did not change after the passage of Bill C-51, it appears that switching of methods for homicide occurred. Leenaars and Lester (2001) extended this preliminary report. They noted that the total homicide rate and the homicide rates by firearms and by all other methods were all increasing in the period 1969-1976 (b = 0.10, 0.05 and 0.08, respectively), but after the passage of Bill C-51, for the period 1978-1985, all three rates stayed at the same level.

Leenaars and Lester (1996) looked at these effects by sex. For male victims, the passage of Bill C-51 led to a reduced use of firearms for homicide and a greater use of all other methods. However, the use of firearms for murdering men stopped increasing after 1977 (as seen from the non-significant regression coefficients). For female victims, the firearms homicide rate decreased after the passage of Bill C-51, with no evidence of switching to other methods for homicide. Furthermore, the percentage of women killed with firearms declined after the passage of Bill C-51. In summary, the passage of Bill C-51 seems to have a more beneficial impact on female victims than on male victims.

As was noted above, Carrington (1999), commenting on an earlier report by Leenaars and Lester (1996) looked at the slopes of the regression lines before and after the passage of Bill C-51, for suicide and for homicide and for both combined and for males and females separately. Most of the trends in homicide prior to the passage of Bill C-51 were positive (increasing rates) and statistically significant. Afterwards, most of the slopes were negative and the changes were significant. For both men and women, there was no evidence for switching methods.

Leenaars and Lester (1997b, 2001) looked at the effects of Bill C-51 by the age of the victim. Comparing the periods 1969-1976 and 1978-1985, the percentage of homcides by firearms decreased for all age groups, significantly so for five of the seven age groups. The firearm homicide rate declined also for all age groups, significantly for five of the seven age groups. However, the homicide rate by all other methods increased only for those 54 years of age or younger while declining for those aged 55+, although not significantly so. The total homicide rates declined for all groups, but significantly so for only those aged 55-64. Thus, switching of methods appears to have taken place for homicide victims under the age of 54, but not for those 55 years of age and older. The linear trends for the two time periods by the age of the homicide victim were inconsistent. However, none of the regression coefficients for the firearm homicide rate by the age of the victim were significantly different from zero, indicating no consistent significant trends within each period even though the average homicide rate dropped for the first period (1969-1976) to the second period (1978-1985).

As noted above, during this time period, many social changes were taking place in Canada aside from changes in gun control laws. Leenaars and Lester (2001; Leenaars & Lester, 1999) ran multiple regressions for the period 1969-1985 using the passage of Bill C-51 (as a dichotomous variable), the percentage of young men aged 15-24, the birth rate, the marriage rate, the divorce rate, the unemployment rate and the median family income to predict the homicide rates by method. In full multiple regressions, the regression coefficient for Bill C-51 was negative for the total homicide rate, the rate by firearm, the rate by all other methods and the percentage of homicides using firearms, but statistically significant only for the total homicide rate. The results by sex (of the victim) were similar, except that, for men, the negative regression coefficient for the percentage of homicides using firearms was also significant along with that for the total homicide rate.

Bridges (2004) explored the impact of two later gun control laws, Bill C-17 (passed in 1991) and Bill C-68 (passed in 1995) on the homicide rate, using the same technique as Leenaars and Lester. Bridges compared the time periods 1984-1990 and 1991-1998. After 1990, the homicide rate using firearms declined, but so did the overall homicide rate and the homicide rate by all other methods. The percentage of homicides using firearms did not change significantly. After 1990, all three homicide rates continued to decline significantly. These results appear to indicate other social forces impacting on homicide rates other than the passage of gun control laws.

Mauser and Holmes (1992) used panel data—for nine of the ten provinces for each year from 1968 to 1988. The association of the passage of Bill C-51 in 1977 was associated with a decline in the homicide rate but not significantly. A multiple regression analysis with five other variables (such as the proportion of males aged 15-24 and the unemployment rate) showed that the effect of the gun control law was statistically significant. However, Mauser and Holmes noted that the homicide rate was declining in Canada from 1973 on and, to correct for that, they added a time variable (year). After this correction, the effect of the gun control law in the multiple regression was no longer statistically significant. Mauser and Holmes concluded that the passage of Bill C-51 had no impact on the homicide rate in Canada.

Accidental Deaths

Leenaars and Lester (1997) examined the impact of Bill C-51 on accidental deaths from firearms for men and women separately. The accidental death rate from firearms decreased in 1969-1976 after the passage of Bill C-51 for both men and women. Males showed a decreasing trend in mortality both before (1969-1976) and after (1978-1985) the passage of Bill C-51, while females showed a decreasing trend only after passage of the bill. To explore the impact of unemployment and divorce rates, these two variables, along with before-versus-after the passage of Bill C-51, were entered into a multiple regression. The impact of the bill was negative on the accidental mortality rate as expected (b = -1.38 for men and -0.32 for women) but not statistically significant.

Leenaars and Lester (1999) ran a multiple regression for the period 1969-1985 using divorce and unemployment rates and the passage of Bill C-51 to predict the accidental mortality from firearms. All three predictor variables were negative and statistically significant, indicating the gun control law reduced accidental mortality from firearms even after controls for divorce and unemployment rates.

Armed Robbery

Mauser and Maki (2003) formed a panel data set (pooled time series and cross-sectional data) for all ten Canadian provinces and the two territories for an 18-year period. In an econometric multiple regression analysis, with nine independent variables, the passage of Bill C-51 did not have a significant impact on the rates of robbery, armed robbery or firearm robbery.

THE IMPLEMENTATION OF GUN CONTROL LAWS

Laws may be passed, but they may not be obeyed or enforced. Lavoie et al. (1994) evaluated the enforcement of Bill C-17 in Quebec. In a random community survey, they found that 99.6% of the firearms were kept unloaded, 70% were inoperative (that is, they had a locking mechanism) or inaccessible (locked up), and 91% had the ammunition safely stored. Sixty-five percent of gun owners had followed all three criteria.

DISCUSSION

This chapter has reviewed a large number of papers, the majority of which are based on the same limited set of data, most of which are shown in Table 7.1. Thus, the differences in the conclusions of the studies depend mostly on the statistical technique used and the subgroup of the Canadian population studied.

All of the studies are, by necessity, correlational, and so cause-and-effect conclusions cannot be drawn. However, nations rarely, if ever, introduce changes in public policy in a way that permits an experimental design. This could be done, for example, by introducing a change in public policy in some regions but not in others. (Ideally, the two sets of regions should be chosen randomly.) Political reality prevents such experiments.

The Canadian situation is complicated by the passage of several gun control bills (in 1968, 1977, 1991 and 1995). During this time period, many social and economic changes also occurred, thereby complicating and possibly confounding the impact of any one variable.

The results are also complicated by the technique of analysis used. In a meta-analysis of studies on the impact of executions on the homicide rate, Yang and Lester (2008) found that the conclusions were different for time-series, ecological and panel data sets. The studies reviewed in this essay on gun control have employed all three methodologies and, therefore, it would not be surprising if the results depended on the methodology used.

For studies of gun control, it is also important to explore the enforcement of the laws. In the study of the deterrent effect of the death penalty, in the 1970s, the focus switched from the study of the existence or passage of a death penalty law to the study of the impact of actual executions. Only one study was identified that explored whether Canadians obey the gun control laws, and no studies were identified on the enforcement of the gun control laws.

One conclusion from this body of research is that gun control appears to reduce the use of firearms for suicide and murder. The evidence as to whether individuals switch to other means for killing themselves or murdering others is contradictory. The conclusion depended on the time period studied, the methodology used, and the particular subgroup of the population that is the focus of the study. The results for studies of suicide and homicide are summarized in Table 7.2. It can be seen that, overall, the gun control laws decreased the use of firearms for suicide and homicide, although not for every subgroup of the population. The different analyses were split almost 50:50 on whether switching to other methods for suicide and murder occurred.

Table 7.2. A summary of the studies of the impact of gun availability on suicide and homicide

	Reducing Firearm Mortality Rates	Did Switching Methods Occur?
Suicide		
Lester (1994)	yes	yes
Lester (2000b)	yes	yes
Bridges & Kunselman (2004)	yes	yes
Simon et al. (1996)	yes	?
Carrington & Moyer (1994b)	yes	no
Effect of gun control laws		
Rich et al. (1990)	no	-
Lester & Leenaars (1993, 1994)	yes	no
Carrington & Moyer (1994a)	yes	no
Carrington & Moyer (1994b)	yes	no
Leenaars & Lester (1996)		
Men	yes	yes
Women	no	-
Leenaars & Lester (1997b)		
15-34 years	no	-
35-64 years	yes	no
65+ years	no	-
Carrington (1999)	yes	no
Leenaars et al. (2003)		
Men	yes	yes
Women	yes	no
Bridges (2004)	yes	yes
Caron (2004)	yes	yes
Caron et al. (2008)	yes	yes
Homicide		
Lester (2000b)	yes	yes
Bridge & Kunselman (2004)	yes	?
Effect of gun control laws		
Leenaars & Lester (1996)		
Men	yes	yes
Women	yes	no
Carrington (1999)	yes	no
Leenaars & Lester (2001)	yes	yes
< 54 years	yes	yes
55+ years	yes	no
Bridges (2004)	yes	no

Public policy is rarely made on the basis of social science research. However, an examination of the situation in Canada suggests that both opponents and advocates of gun control could agree on provisions such as the safe storage of firearms and safety training for those who purchase and own guns. The provision of licenses for purchasing and registering a gun is more controversial, but the requirements that people obtain licenses to drive cars and that cars must be registered do not have any significant impact on people's ownership of cars. Objections to similar requirements for firearms seem to rest on fears of a "slippery slope," that is, that passing such requirements is just the first step to much more stringent requirements. Similarly, restrictions on the type of firearm permitted are reasonable. After all, it is unlikely that any government would permit citizens to own missile launchers and missiles. The difficulty is in negotiating what firearms are allowed and which are not, and assuaging fears of a "slippery slope" in this area.

REFERENCES

Bridges, F. S. (2002). Gun availability and use of guns for murder and suicide in Canada. *Psychological Reports*, 90, 1257-1258.

Bridges, F. S. (2004). Gun control law (Bill C-17), suicide, and homicide in Canada. *Psychological Reports*, 94, 819-826.

Bridges, F. S., & Kunselman, J. C. (2004). Gun availability and use of guns for suicide, homicide, and murder in Canada. *Perceptual & Motor Skills*, 98, 594-598.

Caron, J. (2004). Gun control and suicide. *Archives of Suicide Research*, 8, 361-374.

Caron, J., Julien, M., & Huang, J. H. (2008). Changes in suicide methods in Quebec between 1987 and 2000. *Suicide & Life-Threatening Behavior*, 38, 195-208.

Carrington, P. J. (1999). Gender, gun control, suicide and homicide in Canada. *Archives of Suicide Research*, 5, 71-75.

Carrington, P. J., & Moyer, S. (1994a). Gun control and suicide in Ontario. *American Journal of Psychiatry*, 151, 606-608.

Carrington, P. J., & Moyer, S. (1994b). Gun availability and suicide in Canada. *Studies on Crime & Crime Prevention*, 3, 168-178.

Centerwall, B. S. (1991). Homicide and the prevalence of handguns. *American Journal of Epidemiology*, 134, 1245-1260.

Chapdelaine, A., & Maurice, P. (1996). Firearms injury prevention and gun control in Canada. *Canadian Medical Association Journal*, 155, 1285-1289.

Chapdelaine, A., Samson, E., Kimberley, M. D., & Viau, L. (1991). Firearm-related injuries in Canada. *Canadian Medical Association Journal*, 145, 1217-1223.

Cook, P. J. (1982). The role of firearms in violent crime. In M. E. Wolfgang & M. E. Weiner (Eds.) *Criminal violence*, pp. 236-291. Beverly Hills, CA: Sage.

Cukier, W. (2000). Firearms regulation. *Chronic Diseases in Canada*, 19(1), 25-34.

Finley, C. J., Hemenway, D., Clifton, J., Brown, D. R., Simons, R. K., & Hameed, S. M. (2008). The demographics of significant firearm injury in Canadian trauma centers and the associated predictors of inhospital mortality. *Canadian Journal of Surgery*, 51, 197-203.

Gabor, T. (2003). Universal firearm registration in Canada: Three perspectives. *Canadian Journal of Criminology & Criminal Justice*, 45, 465-471.

Gabor, T., Roberts, J. V., Stein, K., & DiGiulio, L. (2001). Unintentional firearms deaths. *Canadian Journal of Public Health*, 92, 396-398.

Hung, C. K. (1993). Comments on the article…"Gun control and rates of firearms violence in Canada and the United States" by Robert J. Mundt. *Canadian Journal of Criminology*, 35, 37-41.

Lavoie, M. Cardinal, L., Chapdelaine, A., & St-Laurent, D. (1994). L'état d'entreposage des armes à feu longues gardées à domicile au Quebec. *Maladies Chroniques au Canada*, 22, 26-32.

Leenaars, A. A., & Lester, D. (1992). Comparison of rates and patterns of suicide in Canada and the United States, 1960-1988. *Death Studies*, 16, 417-430.

Leenaars, A. A., & Lester, D. (1994a). Suicide and homicide rates in Canada and the United States. *Suicide & Life-Threatening Behavior*, 24, 184-191.

Leenaars, A. A., & Lester, D. (1994b). Effects of gun control on homicide in Canada. *Psychological Reports*, 75, 81-82.

Leenaars, A. A., & Lester, D. (1996). Gender and the impact of gun control on suicide and homicide. *Archives of Suicide Research*, 2, 223-234.

Leenaars, A. A., & Lester, D. (1997a). The effects of gun control on the accidental death rate from firearms in Canada. *Journal of Safety Research*, 28, 119-122.

Leenaars, A. A., & Lester, D. (1997b). The impact of gun control on suicide and homicide across the life span. *Canadian Journal of Behavioural Sciences*, 29, 1-6.

Leenaars, A. A., & Lester, D. (1999). Gender, gun control, suicide and homicide. *Archives of Suicide Research*, 5, 77-79.

Leenaars, A. A., & Lester, D. (2001). The impact of gun control (Bill C-51) on homicide in Canada. *Journal of Criminal Justice*, 29, 287-294.

Leenaars, A. A., Moksony, F., Lester, D., & Wenckstern, S. (2003). The impact of gun control (Bill C-51) on suicide in Canada. *Death Studies*, 27, 103-124.

Lester, D. (1984). *Gun control: Issues and answers*. Springfield, IL: Charles Thomas.

Lester, D. (1990). The availability of firearms and the use of firearms for suicide. *Acta Psychiatrica Scandinavica*, 81, 146-147.

Lester, D. (1994). Use of firearms for suicide in Canada. *Perceptual & Motor Skills*, 79, 962.

Lester, D. (2000a). Armed robbery and the availability of firearms in Canada. *EuroCriminology*, 14, 113-115.

Lester, D. (2000b). Gun availability and the use of guns for suicide and homicide in Canada. *Canadian Journal of Public Health*, 91, 186-187.

Lester, D. (2001). Gun availability and use of guns for murder and suicide in Canada. *Psychological Reports*, 89, 624.

Lester, D., & Leenaars, A. A. (1993). Suicide rates in Canada before and after tightening firearm control laws. *Psychological Reports*, 72, 787-790.

Lester, D., & Leenaars, A. A. (1994). Gun control and rates of firearms violence in Canada and the United States. *Canadian Journal of Criminology*, 36, 463-464.

Lester, D., & Leenaars, A. A. (1998). Is there a regional subculture of firearm violence in Canada? *Medicine, Science & the Law*, 38, 317-320.

Mauser, G. A. (1990). A comparison of Canadian and American attitudes towards firearms. *Canadian Journal of Criminology*, 32, 573-589.

Mauser, G. A. (1996). Armed self-defense. *Journal of Criminal Justice*, 24, 393-406.

Mauser, G. A, & Holmes, R. A. (1992). An evaluation of the 1977 Canadian firearms legislation. *Evaluation Review*, 16, 603-617.

Mauser, G. A., & Maki, D. (2003). An evaluation of the 1977 Canadian firearm legislation. *Applied Economics*, 35, 423-436.

Mauser, G. A., & Margolis, M. (1992). The politics of gun control. *Government & Policy*, 10, 189-209.

Miller, T. R. (1995). Costs associated with gunshot wounds in Canada in 1991. *Canadian Medical Association Journal*, 153, 1261-1268.

Mundt, R. J. (1990). Gun control and rates of firearms violence in Canada and the United States. *Canadian Journal of Criminology*, 32, 137-154.

Quan, H., & Arboleda-Florez, J. (1999). Elderly suicide in Alberta. *Canadian Journal of Psychiatry*, 44, 762-768.

Rich, C. L., Young, J. G., Fowler, R. C., Wagner, J., & Black, N. A. (1990). Guns and suicide. *American Journal of Psychiatry*, 147, 342-346.

Simon, R., Chouinard, M., & Gravel, C. (1996). Suicide and firearms. In J. L. McIntosh (Ed.) *Suicide '96*, pp.35-37. Washington, DC: American Association of Suicidology.

Sloan, J. H., Kellerman, A. L., Reay, D. T., Ferris, J. A., Koepsell, T., Rivara, F. P., Rice, C., Gray, L., & LoGerfo, J. (1988). Handgun regulations, crime, assaults, and homicide. *New England Journal of Medicine*, 319, 1256-1262.

Sloan, J. H., Rivara, F. P., Reay, D. T., Ferris, J. A., & Kellerman, A. L. (1990). Firearm regulations and rates of suicide. *New England Journal of Medicine*, 322, 369-373.

Sproule, C. F., & Kennett, D. J. (1988). The use of firearms in Canadian homicides 1972-1982. *Canadian Journal of Criminology*, 30, 31-37.

Sproule, C. F., & Kennett, D. J. (1989). Killing with guns in the USA and Canada 1977-1983. *Canadian Journal of Criminology*, 31, 245-251.

Yang, B., & Lester, D. (2008). The deterrent effect of executions. *Journal of Criminal Justice*, 36, 453-460.

Chapter 8

GUN CONTROL IN AUSTRALIA AND OTHER COUNTRIES

Occasional research on the impact of access to firearms has been conducted in other nations, such as Australia, which is of interest because attitudes toward guns and gun control differ by nation. For example, in a survey of college students, Cooke (2004) found that students in Australia and the United Kingdom scored lower on questions measuring whether they favored gun possession, on whether people have a right to own a gun, and whether possession of a gun provides protection from crime. They scored higher on the belief that guns stimulate crime.

The role of gun control and gun availability in Australia is of particular interest because the country moved from having individual state and territory laws prior to 1996 to a nationwide gun control law thereafter.

STUDIES IN AUSTRALIA PRIOR TO 1996

Lester (1988) studied six Australian states in 1975–1977 and correlated the number of guns per capita and the percentage of households owning guns with the suicide rate and the homicide rate. For males, the more guns in the state, the higher the firearm suicide rate, the lower the suicide rate by all other methods and the higher the percentages of suicides using guns. For homicide, the more guns in the state, the higher the percentage of homicides using guns. The percentage of households owning guns was more strongly associated with the suicide and homicide measures than was the number of guns per capita. Lester showed that the results for the six Australian states paralleled the results for the nine major regions of the United States for the same period.

Snowdon and Harris (1992) conducted a similar study. They studied suicide in five Australian states for the period 1968 to 1989. (They could not obtain reliable data for the Northern Territories or the Australian Capital Territory, and they omitted Tasmania.) The use of firearms for suicide was primarily a male choice, with male firearm suicide rates in 1989 ranging from 3.8 per 100,000 per year in Western Australia to 8.4 in Queensland. In contrast, the female firearm suicide rate in 1989 ranged from 0.1 in Western Australia to 0.6 in South Australia. Snowdon and Harris had estimates for the percentage of households with guns in 1975 and average annual male firearm suicide rates for 1968 to 1989. The Spearman rank correlation coefficient (calculated by the present author) between the two variables is 0.9, which is statistically significant at the one-tailed 5% level.

Cantor and Lewin (1990) reported a more extensive analysis of the use of guns for suicide in Australia for the period 1961–1985. During this period, the total suicide rate declined, but the firearm suicide rate remained stable, with the result that the proportion of suicides using firearms increased. Young males showed an increasing use of guns for suicide. In their regional analysis, Cantor and Lewin added Tasmania and used measures of guns per 1,000 persons and the percentage of households owning a gun. Both measures were positively (but non-significantly) associated with the proportion of suicides using guns in the six states for males and for females.

During this period, South Australia passed a gun control law in 1977 which was implemented in 1980. This law required gun owners to be licensed and pass an exam on the safety and handling of weapons. The firearms suicide rate in South Australia declined from 1968–1979 to 1980–1989 (from 6.7 to 5.8), whereas it rose in the four other states (from 5.4 to 6.1). However, the suicide rate by all other methods rose in South Australia (from 9.6 to 12.8), as it did in the four other states (from 11.0 to 12.6). The total suicide rate, therefore, rose from 16.3 to 18.6 in South Australia and from 16.4 to 18.7 in the four other states. The question of whether, when gun ownership was restricted, people switched to other methods for suicide cannot easily be answered by these data.

Cantor and Slater (1995) studied Queensland in the two years prior and after passage of a weapons act that required the purchase of a license to buy a long gun, a waiting period, and a safety examination. Pre-existing long gun owners also had to acquire a license. The number of suicides using guns declined significantly for men (very few women used guns for suicide), in those of all ages and in metropolitan areas and provincial cities but not in rural areas. The total number of suicides by men declined also, mainly in the provincial cities.

THE IMPACT OF THE 1996 GUN LAW IN AUSTRALIA

On May 10, 1996, a mass murderer killed 35 people and injured 18 serious in Tasmania. In response, the individual states passed a uniform gun control law which was implemented between 1996 and 1998 (National Firearms Agreement, NFA). The new law banned rapid-fire long guns, required the registration of all guns, required owners to be licensed, banned private firearms sales, and required police approval for the transfer of guns. The government also introduced a buy-back program which netted some 700,000 guns. Reuter and Mouzos (2003) attempted to analyze the impact of the buy-back program and passage of the but, not only did they not employ any statistical techniques (merely charting the trends in suicide and homicide during the period involved) but it is impossible to evaluate the effects of the buy-back program separately from the passage of the gun control laws. Reviewing a number of unpublished studies from the Australian Institute of Criminology, they noted that: (1) firearm-related homicides declined even more sharply after the NFA while the proportion of homicides using guns increased, (2) firearm suicide rates declined before and after the NFA with no noticeable change in the decline after the NRA, (3) accidental firearm injuries declined after the NFA, including hospitalization for such injuries, (4) attempted murder using firearms remained stable and showed little change, (5) while armed robberies increased during the period, the use of guns in those robberies declined after the NFA, and (6) the number of firearms stolen declined after the NFA.

Chapman, Alpers, Agho and Jones (2007) studied the impact of the 1996 national gun control law. They found that:

(1) The rate of total firearm deaths was declining by 3% per year prior to 1996 and by 6% after 1996.
(2) The rate of firearm suicides was declining by 3% per year prior to 1996 and by 7.4% after 1996.
(3) The rate of firearm homicides was declining by 3% per year prior to 1996 and by 7.5% after 1996.
(4) The rate of accidental firearms deaths was declining by 7.6% per year prior to 1996 but *increased* by 8.5% after 1996.

Thus, the 1996 law reduced firearms deaths in suicide and homicide, but not accidental death. This latter phenomena was based on very small numbers of death, and McPhedran and Baker (2008) suggested that it was a result of coroners classifying more suicides as unintentional deaths and, even if the verdict was eventually corrected, the Australian Bureau of Statistics failing to tabulate accurate statistics on deaths (De Leo, 2007).

What of switching to other methods for homicide and suicide? The total non-firearm homicide rate was increasing by 1.1% per year prior to 1996, but declined by 2.4% after 1996. The total homicide rate was stable prior to 1996 and declined after 1996. Thus, no switching of method occurred for homicide.

The non-firearm suicide rate was increasing at 2.3% per year prior to 1996 and declined by 4.1% after 1996. The total suicide rate was stable prior to 1996 and declined after 1996. No evidence was found, therefore, that switching of methods occurred for suicide.

Baker and McPhedran (2007) used a different statistical technique (the ARIMA or Box-Jenkins model) and found that firearm suicide rates declined significantly more than predicted after the passage of the 1996 NFA. The suicide rate by all other methods did not differ from predictions, except for 1997 and 1998 when this rate was higher than expected, but not thereafter. Homicide rates by firearms and by all other methods did not differ from predictions, and so the NFA did not appear to have an impact on homicides. Finally, their analysis showed that the observed rate of accidental firearm death was higher than predicted.

Klieve, Barnes and De Leo (2008) looked at the impact of the 1996 law on male suicide in Australia and in Queensland where a suicide register has been established to monitor suicides more accurately. The results for Queensland and Australia are similar, namely, a steady declining firearm suicide rate from 1990 to 2004, combined with a steadily increasing suicide rate by hanging. Klieve et al. observed that the downward trends in the firearm suicide rate in Queensland in 1990-1996 and 1997-2004 were not significantly different. However, visual inspection of their graphs shows a noticeable discontinuity in the period 1996-1998. Klieve et al. noted that the age of those using hanging declined over the period while the age of those using firearms increased. This suggests that younger males turned to hanging more while older males continued to use firearms.

Ozanne-Smith et al. (2004) reported changes in firearm-related deaths in Victoria as compared to the rest of Australia. Victoria tightened restrictions on semi-automatic guns in 1988, whereas the rest of Australia did not do so. In 1996, along with the other Australian states, Victoria adopted the national firearm standards. From 1988 to 1995, Victoria experienced a 17.3% reduction in firearm deaths relative to Australia, and this was significant for all firearm deaths and for firearm suicides, but not for firearm homicide and unintentional firearm deaths. After 1997, Australia experienced a 14.0% reduction in firearm deaths relative to Victoria, so that Australia as a whole "caught up" with the decline in Victoria.

Incidentally, Ozanne-Smith et al. noted that, in 1998 as compared to 1992, household ownership of guns and ammunition declined in Melbourne, and the number of registered firearms and owners in Victoria also declined. (The buyback program in Australia lasted from September 1996 to September 1997.)

STUDIES RELEVANT TO SWITCHING METHODS FOR SUICIDE IN AUSTRALIA

De Leo, Evans and Neulinger (2002) compared males using hanging, firearms and non-domestic gas (mainly car exhaust) for suicide in Queensland in 1994-1996. They found differences in the personal and social characteristics of the suicides. Those using non-domestic gas more often lived alone and left a suicide note, those using firearms had less often made previous attempts at suicide, while those using hanging were more often psychotic and younger. Thus, different types of people choose the various methods for suicide, and this suggests (but does not prove) that changing the availability of a method for suicide would affect only some sub-groups of the population.

One problem in examining the availability of one single method of suicide over time is that the availability of other methods changes, too. If guns are made less readily available, there may be changes in car ownership and type of car owned, changes in emission controls on cars, changes in the availability and toxicity of domestic gas, fencing in bridges and other high buildings, and restrictions on medications (both prescribed and over-the-counter) and pesticides at the same time. No study has examined changes in the availability of several methods of suicide during the same period of tie.

However, changes in method for suicide have been documented over time. De Leo, Dwyer, Firman and Neulinger (2003) noted that, from 1975 to 1998 in Australia for males, the suicide rate by firearm declined while the suicide rate by hanging increased. The data presented by these authors also showed an increase in the use of "other gases" (that is, car exhaust). The overall male suicide rate increased during this time period. The largest change was the increase in the use of hanging for suicide and, obviously, access to this method for suicide cannot be restricted. De Leo et al. argued that their data showed that substitution of method had occurred in Australia as the availability of guns was restricted.

There have been occasional papers on the impact of gun control in Austria, Brazil England and Wales, and New Zealand.

AUSTRIA

Etzerdorfer et al. (2006) compared the number of gun licenses held in each of nine Austrian counties in the period 1990-2000 with the suicide rate. The association between the firearm license rate and the firearm suicide rate was strong (the correlation was 0.98), and the association with suicide by all other methods was not significantly different from zero, indicating that switching methods was not apparent. The association of the firearm license rate with the total suicide rate was positive but weak (the correlation was 0.38).

Austria adopted a new firearm control law in 1997 with changes in the type and reasons permitted for purchasing a firearm, psychological testing and background checks, a cooling off period, and storage regulations. Kapusta et al. (2007) studied the period 1985-2005 to see how the use of guns for suicide and homicide changed after 1997. Firearm suicides rates were steady prior to 1997 and declined thereafter (and this decline was found after controls for unemployment and alcohol consumption, and for both men and women). A similar decrease in the percentage of suicides using guns was found. During this period, the overall suicide rate declined, and so there was no evidence for switching of methods for suicide. Parallel results were found for homicides using guns, which declined after 1997, as did licenses issued for purchasing guns.

BRAZIL

Brazil passed a set of gun control laws in 2003 and 2004 to cope with the incidence of firearm-related deaths—39,325 in 2003, 90% of which were homicides. The laws required registration of guns, made it illegal to carry guns outside of one's home or business, instituted background checks for purchasers, raised the minimum age for purchase to 25 and instituted tougher sentences for violations. There was also a buy-back program. De Souza et al. (2007) studied the impact of these changes and documented a reverse from an increasing trend in firearm-related deaths to a declining trend after 2003. This decline was found in all major regions of Brazil, but not all smaller subdivisions of the regions experienced the decline, suggesting that enforcement of the laws may have been uneven. There was also a decline in hospitalizations related to firearm injuries after 2003, primarily as a result of a decline in accidental and suicidal firearm injuries (but not as a result of injuries from assaults). De Souza et al. estimated that the passage of the laws averted some 5,563 deaths in Brazil in 2004. Brazilians rejected an outright ban on firearms in 2005.

De Souza et al. presented figures and tables of data without any statistical analyses or controls for other changes over the period. Furthermore, they did not study suicide separately from homicide and did not explore whether switching of methods occurred for either suicide or homicide.

ENGLAND AND WALES

England and Wales passed a gun control law in 1989 regulating the purchase, registration and storage of firearms. Hawton et al. (1998) examined the methods used for suicide by farmers from 1981 to 1993 and noted that the use of firearms declined after 1989, as did the total number of suicides. For all male suicides in England and Wales (excluding the farmers), the firearm suicide rate declined but the overall suicide rate did not change.

NEW ZEALAND

Alpers and Walters (1998) estimated that about 5.5% of the population in New Zealand (about 200,000 licensed owners) owned about one million firearms, nine times more per capita than in England and 20 percent higher than in Australia. For the period 1994–1997, Alpers and Walters searched the media for reports of stolen firearms and located 94 reports. They then sought information from the relevant police districts and obtained data for 88 incidents. While 77% of the guns were stolen from homes, 9% were stolen from cars, 7% from businesses and 6% from farm sheds, indicating poor adherence to safe-storage measures. Insecure storage was present in 52% of the incidents. The stolen guns were primarily long guns (shotguns and rifles) whereas guns obtained illegally are typically handguns. In 23% of the incidents,, the stolen guns were used in subsequent acts of violence or crime (including robberies, murders and kidnappings as well as suicides).

Newbold (1999) surveyed 51 prison inmates who had been convicted either of a crime involving a gun (82%) or of illegal possession of a firearm. The most popular weapon was a shotgun (42%), followed by pistols (24%) and sporting rifles (23%). Seventy-one percent of the shotguns had the barrel and/or butt sawed off. Only 26% of the guns had been stolen, the rest being obtained from relatives, friends or acquaintances.

Gun Control in New Zealand

In New Zealand, after a mass murderer killed 13 people with a semi-automatic weapon in 1990, a gun control law was passed in 1992, and implemented in 1993–1996. The law required photo-ID licenses to own a gun, passing a test of knowledge of the firearm code and of firearm safety, assessment by police, and storage requirements.

Beautrais, Fergusson and Horwood (2006) noted that the firearm suicide rate declined from pre-implementation to implementation to post-implementation, overall and for those of all ages. The percentage of suicides using firearms declined from 18% to 10% from pre- to post-implementation. However, there were no significant changes in the total suicide rate after implementation, nor in the suicide rate of youths and adults, suggesting that switching of methods for suicide occurred.

In an earlier study, Beautrais, Joyce and Mulder (1996) compared 150 suicides in Canterbury, New Zealand, with 302 serious suicide attempters. Twenty of the completed suicides (13.3%) and four of the attempted suicide (1.3%) used firearms. Of the 452 suicidal individuals, 22 of the 24 using guns had access to a gun (91.7%) as compared to only 43 of the 428 suicidal individuals using other methods (1.0%), a significant difference. Thus, access to a gun was associated with a suicidal individual choosing a gun for their suicidal action. However, compared to 1028 community control subjects, the suicides were not more likely to have access to a gun, even when age and the presence of a psychiatric disorder was controlled for. Thus, having access to a gun did not seem to increase the risk of suicide.

COMMENT

There has been far less research on the impact of access to firearms in the five countries discussed in this chapter, but the results parallel those found for Canada in Chapter 7. Restricting access to guns does reduce their use for suicide and for homicide, but the evidence for whether individuals switch methods is incocnsistent.

REFERENCES

Alpers, P., & Walters, R. (1998). Firearms theft in New Zealand. *Australian & New Zealand Journal of Criminology*, 31, 85-95.

Baker, J., & McPhedran, S. (2007). Gun laws and sudden death. *British Journal of Criminology*, 47, 455-469.

Beautrais, A. L., Fergusson, D. M., & Horwood, L. J. (2006). Firearms legislation and reductions in firearm-related suicide deaths in New Zealand. *Australian & New Zealand Journal of Psychiatry*, 40, 253-259.

Beautrais, A. L., Joyce, P. R., & Mulder, R. T. (1996). Access to firearms and the risk of suicide. *Australian & New Zealand Journal of Psychiatry*, 30, 741-748.

Cantor, C. H., & Slater, P. J. (1995). The impact of firearm control legislation on suicide in Queensland. *Medical Journal of Australia*, 162, 583-585.

Cantor, C. H.. & Lewin, T. (1990). Firearms and suicide in Australia. *Australian & New Zealand Journal of Psychiatry*, 24, 500-509.

Chapman, S., Alpers, P., Agho, K., & Jones, M. (2007). Australia's 1996 gun law reforms. *Injury Prevention*, 12, 365-372.

Cooke, C. A. (2004). Young people's attitudes towards guns in America, Great Britain, and Western Australia. *Aggressive Behavior*, 30, 93-104.

De Leo, D. (2007). Suicide mortality data needs revision. *Medical Journal of Australia*, 186, 157.

De Leo, D., Dwyer, J., Firman, D., & Neulinger, K. (2003). Trends in hanging and firearm suicide rates in Australia. *Suicide & Life-Threatening Behavior*, 33, 151-164.

De Leo, D., Evans, R., & Neulinger, K. (2002). Hanging, firearm, and non-domestic gas suicides among males. *Australian & New Zealand Journal of Psychiatry*, 36, 183-189.

De Souza, M, Macinko, J., Alencar, A. P., Malta, D. C., & de Morais Neto, O. L. (2007). Reductions in firearm-related mortality and hospitalizations in Brazil after gun control. *Health Affairs*, 26, 575-584.

Etzerdorfer, E., Kapusta, N. D., & Sonneck, G. (2006). Suicide by shooting is correlated to the rate of gun licenses in Austrian counties. *Wiener Klinische Wochenschrift*, 118, 464-468.

Hawton, K., Fagg, J., Simkin, S., Harris, L., & Malmberg, A. (1998). Methods used for suicide by farmers in England and Wales. *British Journal of Psychiatry*, 173, 320-324.

Kapusta, N. D., Etzerdorfer, E., Krall, C., & Sonneck, G. (2007). Firearm legislation reform in the European Union. *British Journal of Psychiatry*, 191,253-257.

Klieve, H., Barnes, M., & De Leo, D. (2008). Controlling firearms use in Australia. *Social Psychiatry & Psychiatric Epidemiology*, 44, 285-292.

Lester, D. (1988). Restricting the availability of guns as a strategy for preventing suicide. *Biology & Society*, 5, 127-129.

McPhedran, S., & Baker, J. (2008). Australian firearms legislation and unintentional firearm deaths. *Journal of Public Health*, 122, 297-299.

Newbold, G. (1999). The criminal use of firearms in New Zealand. *Australian & New Zealand Journal of Criminology*, 32, 61-78.

Ozanne-Smith, J., Ashby, K., Newstead, S., Stathakis, V. Z., & Clapperton, A. (2004). Firearm related deaths. *Injury Prevention*, 10, 280-286.

Reuter, P., & Mouzos, J. (2003). Australia. In J. Ludwig & P. J. Cook (Eds.) *Evaluating gun policy*, pp. 121-156. Washington, DC: Brookings Institute Press.

Snowdon, J., & Harris, L. (1992). Firearms suicides in Australia. *Medical Journal of Australia*, 156, 79-88.

Chapter 9

CONCLUSION

The research reviewed in this book leads to a clear conclusion. *Severely restricting* access to a lethal method for suicide reduces its use for suicide. The research on the impact of the switch from toxic coal gas (with a high level of carbon monoxide) to natural gas eliminated the use of domestic gas as a method for suicide. Fencing in a suicide venue from which people jump to their death (such as a bridge or a subway station) removes that venue as an option for suicides. There can be no dispute about this.

What is the impact of *limiting* access to a lethal method for suicide? If car exhaust is made less toxic (through the use of catalytic converters which lower the level of carbon monoxide in the gas), but not completely non-toxic, does this have an impact on the use of car exhaust for suicide? If a strict gun control law is passed which does not greatly impact the level of ownership of guns in a society, does this reduce the use of guns for suicide?

Here the evidence is less clear. With regard to car exhaust, some countries experienced a decline in the use of that method for suicide as a greater proportion of cars were fitted with catalytic converters, while others did not. The evidence for the impact of a stricter gun control law is even more inconsistent, with researchers drawing different conclusions from the same data set (in the present book, using data from Canada, for example). In general the research reviewed in this book suggests that, overall, limiting access to a lethal method for suicide (rather than eliminating it) usually reduces the use of that method for suicide.

The evidence regarding switching methods for suicide is also unclear. For some methods, such as the impact of gun control laws, the research is inconsistent. For other methods, such as the detoxification of domestic gas, the increasing use of car exhaust seems to have occurred in some countries. For a method such as medications or pesticides, restricting the availability of one substance often leads to an alternative substance (medication or pesticide) taking its place. This switch does not always occur immediately (as, for example, in the case of domestic gas and car exhaust in England), but it may occur eventually.

In order to explore this problem more thoroughly, it is important that research be conducted on individuals. How many people do switch methods as they make a series of non-fatal attempts at suicide? What are the most common switches in method, that is, if domestic gas or car exhaust is not available, do those whose who switch have a preferred alternative method? What distinguishes those who switch methods from those who do not? This research has not yet been carried out.

The answers to these questions are important when we consider whether restricting access to a lethal method for suicide has an impact on the overall suicide rate (using all methods combined). The research on the detoxification of domestic gas provided a reasonable answer to this. When domestic gas was a very popular method for suicide in a country, the detoxification of domestic gas was accompanied by a reduction in the overall suicide rate. When domestic gas was an uncommon method for suicide in a country, the detoxification of domestic gas had no impact on the overall suicide rate.

If restricting access to a lethal method for suicide has no impact on the overall suicide rate, is it worth restricting access to that method? I have always found this question odd because it is never asked in other areas of public health. Government agencies concerned with occupational health and safety remove all hazards from the workplace regardless of whether they save a few lives or many. A medication can be withdrawn if only a few people die from the side-effects regardless of how many people are saved from illness or death for which the medication was designed. In these areas, saving one life is considered to be important. In suicide, saving one life is rarely considered to be as important.

This point is illustrated by the objection to fencing in bridges from which suicides jump to their death because of esthetic reasons! I put an exclamation point at the end of that sentence because it is amazing to me that those who object on esthetic grounds put so little value on saving lives.

Some critics of situational suicide prevention often bring up the possibility that people will switch methods for suicide as an argument for not fencing in the bridge (or restricting other methods for suicide). In the United States, the requirement that backyard swimming pools be fenced in to prevent accidents is not affected by the possibility that people may drown themselves accidentally in lakes, rivers and the oceans. Making the environment safe is a worthy goal even if it cannot be made absolutely safe.

It is noteworthy that the major movements to restrict access to lethal methods for suicide have typically been made on cost or environmental grounds. The use of emission controls on cars was motivated by efforts to reduce pollution. The change from toxic coal gas to less toxic natural gas for domestic use was prompted by cost and pollution considerations. Preventing suicide was not a primary consideration. In contrast, efforts to reduce the widespread availability of pesticides has been motivated by efforts to prevent their use for suicide and accidental deaths.

THE ROLE OF IMPULSIVITY

In setting up telephone crisis intervention services, part of the rational was suicidal crises are often time-limited. Helping individuals in crisis to get through the night or the next few days may find them in a less suicidal mood later and, thereby, save their lives. Many suicidal actions (fatal and non-fatal) are made impulsively.[1] It takes time to string up a rope in one's garage. It takes time to die from inhaling car exhaust or from an overdose of a medication. Many people change their minds and call for help or are saved by passers-by. In contrast, a suicidal individual who has a loaded gun in their home can find it quickly and use it impulsively to commit suicide.

We need much more research on the role of impulsivity in suicidal actions. How many suicidal individuals act impulsively? What is the time between deciding to commit suicide and actually using the method chosen? How do impulsive suicides differ from non-impulsive suicides in personality, precipitating circumstances, psychiatric status, etc? Are the actions of those using guns for suicide more impulsive than those who use medications or not? There is very little research on these questions.

IMPLICATIONS FOR A THEORY OF SUICIDE

The research reviewed in this book and the answers to the questions raised above have implications for a theory of suicide. For example, if some individuals would not switch methods for suicide if their preferred method for suicide was not

---

[1] It should be noted that many non-fatal suicide attempts often result in serious and permanent physical harm to the person.

available, what does this say about their intent to die? Would different variables precipitate suicide in those who would switch and those who would not? Would different theories of suicide be applicable to these two groups?

If some individuals have a preferred method for suicide, what determines this preference? There is a great of research, some of which was reviewed in the chapters in this book, on simple demographic differences (by age and sex, for example) in those using different methods for suicide, but almost no research on the psychodynamics and personality of those choosing different methods.

Clearly, not only has the research reviewed in this book indicated that situational suicide prevention—closing the exits—can save lives, but it has identified an important research agenda for suicidologists in the future.

INDEX

H

I

N

O

P

T